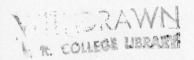

THE HYMN AND CONGREGATIONAL SINGING

James Rawlings Sydnor

The Hymn
and
Congregational
Singing

John Knox Press
RICHMOND, VIRGINIA

Library of Congress Catalog Card Number: 60-9708

ML
3111
.S95
1960
Sept 2001
AAT 2870

Preface

This book was born of the conviction that the greatest single musical contribution which church leaders could make to their individual congregations would be in the development of superior congregational singing. It is the purpose of this volume to provide orderly guidance in the transfer of the treasures of the hymnal to the hearts and lips and lives of every Christian. Its aim is to enable as many Christians as possible to reproduce in their lives the same measure of devotion and spiritual insight enjoyed by the writers of the great hymns. This re-enactment may occur in the private or public devotions of the individuals. Every sincere motion in this direction will be aided by the gracious assistance of the Holy Spirit.

Hymn singing is rooted in the knowledge that man can communicate with his Creator and can share in this devotion with his fellow worshipers. It presupposes the priesthood of the individual believer. It is based on the assumption, stated ages ago by the Psalmist, that all the people should praise God. Since this is so, the Church has generally provided hymns of such simplicity and worth that the lowliest saint could lift his heart in praise.

The quality of hymn singing in American churches varies considerably from denomination to denomination and from congregation to congregation. There is room for further growth even in churches which are noted for excellent singing. At the other extreme are congregations which stand mainly mute during the playing of hymns, almost completely unawakened to the joys and inner satisfactions of the corporate praise of God. Let us hope that there are none which merit the description given by John Wesley of the psalm singing in some town churches of his day. He wrote that "the miserable, scandalous doggerel . . . was bawled out by a handful of wild, unawakened striplings who neither feel nor understand" what they "scream," while the congregation was "lolling at ease, or in the indecent posture of sitting, drawling out one word after another."

5

Congregational song in American churches—in the opinion of many observers, clerical and musical—is respectable but far from the realization of its full possibilities. Analogically speaking, it does little good to have a superb collection of art in the local gallery if the public has never been induced to come and absorb the beauty and interest inherent in the works of art.

The materials for stimulating a magnificent outburst of singing among Christians across this broad land have never been as plentiful as now or of such high caliber. There is scarcely a denomination which has not during the past generation issued standard hymnals which contain between their covers many of the best hymns, ancient and modern. The ministry generally is more cognizant of the latent possibilities of vital hymn singing and yearns to loose the springs of song. Church musicians are increasingly widening their interests to include the music in the pews as a major concern. And the winds of God are sweeping through the hearts of thousands of laymen everywhere. Their desire for stability in things spiritual, their gratitude to their Creator and Preserver, and their concern for doing the truth in daily life—each of these impulses is a subject for Christian hymnody.

Furthermore, a hymnological literature of amazing breadth and scholarship has evolved. Numerous handbooks of hymnals give accurate background material about hymn texts and tunes, authors and composers. Solid technical studies of the music of hymns have recently appeared. Narratives—long and short—of the Church's song through the ages may be read. Scholars have made studies of the philosophy, theology, and aesthetics of hymnody.

To this impressive literature, I would like to add this manual on the thoughtful ordering of congregational praise because there is considerable disparity between the content of our superior hymnals and the quality of hymn singing in congregations served by these hymnals. It has been said that a hymn is not really a good hymn until it has been well written, well chosen, and well sung. In these pages I have attempted to analyze the factors which produce truly great congregational singing and to do it in a nontechnical manner so that the disclosure may be readily understood. I have tried to keep in mind ministers and laymen who have little or no musical background.

Illustrations of texts and tunes referred to in this manual usually may be found in either *The Hymnbook* (published in 1955 jointly by five Presbyterian or Reformed bodies in the United States) or in *The Hymnal* 1940 of the Protestant Episcopal Church in the United States of America. The former is indicated by the letter P; the latter by the letter E.

The Editors of *The Presbyterian Outlook,* in which some of the following material originally appeared, have graciously granted permission to include it in this volume.

CONTENTS

PART SIX

EDUCATING THE CONGREGATION
TO SING HYMNS

Part One

INTRODUCTION

CHAPTER 1
Who Is Responsible for Improving Congregational Singing?

There are many springs and tributaries feeding the stream of praise which issues from the hearts and voices of a congregation assembled for worship on a Sunday morning. Any experience which deepens the spiritual life of the people will be reflected in increased vitality of praise. Paul told the Colossians to let the word of Christ dwell in their hearts, and in the same sentence he reminded them to sing psalms and hymns with thankfulness.

The devout Christian who in private devotions draws his personal copy of the hymnal from the table and meditates on some beloved hymn is contributing to congregational praise, because hymns must be appropriated privately before corporate praise can become fully intelligent. A family which bows before a meal to sing the Doxology or some familiar stanza like "For the beauty of the earth" will have increased interest in these stanzas when they are sung in church. A mother humming "Joyful, joyful, we adore Thee" while doing housework deepens the spirit of praise in that church. An informal hymn-sing in a home or in the church parlor on Sunday evening when people call out their old favorites is an ideal way of cultivating confidence in song.

We must not limit our concept of the function of hymns solely to their utterance three times on Sunday morning. Those readers who saw the motion picture "How Green Was My Valley" will recall the remarkable way in which hymns were used in Wales to express many of the emotions of everyday life. We heard the miners striding home at the end of a work day, singing the Welsh hymn tune Cwm Rhondda. Especially moving was the scene by

13

the mine entrance after an explosion when the villagers were waiting for the elevator to bring up the bodies of their loved ones.
They comforted each other by singing a poignant hymn of faith.

Who, then, is responsible for developing congregational singing? Every single individual in the congregation! The man or woman in the pew who sings heartily and thoughtfully every time a
hymn is announced is directly promoting this musical offering.
The church school teacher who, when teaching about Christian
brotherhood, opens the hymnal perhaps to "In Christ there is no
East or West" and explains its meaning is improving hymn singing. The Sunday school superintendent who chooses hymns carefully according to the needs of the pupils, rather than according
to his own past favorites, is fulfilling his responsibility. The children's choir director who has a project of hymn notebooks for
his children to stimulate them to learn the stories and to memorize
the texts is helping to improve corporate praise.

Obviously the more influential post an individual has, the
greater is his responsibility. Sharing the greatest responsibility
are the leader in worship and the hymn player. In the services of
the whole congregation these persons usually are the minister
and the organist. There are many specific practical suggestions
which can be given these two important individuals. However,
we must also remember the part which a choir can play in influencing congregational singing. The Music Committee will consider this area of church music its prime responsibility. And, most
important, we must direct considerable attention to the man in
the pew. He must be educated in methods of fulfilling his responsibility in musical praise.

CHAPTER **2** The Values of
Congregational Singing

For more than nineteen centuries Christians have sung hymns.
Why? In the upper room, in the catacombs, in monastery chapels,
vast cathedrals, camp meeting tents, conference auditoriums, vil-
lage churches, city sanctuaries, hymns of prayer and praise have
risen from the hearts of countless Christians.

Why? What values are there in the simple act of singing hymns
which have caused the Church to bind its songs close to its heart?
There are at least five reasons why Christians sing hymns.

1. *Through hymn singing, Christians express their feelings and
ideas.* Our Protestant concept of worship has at its center the
priesthood of the individual believer. Therefore, the individual
Christian in worship holds converse with his Creator. In the ideal
service of worship, patterned frequently after Isaiah's in his sixth
chapter, the Christian passes through a series of emotional experiences—awe, contrition, illumination, and consecration. These and
many other feelings, aroused by a true experience of worship,
need expression and can find ready outlet through hymn singing.
"Holy, Holy, Holy! Lord God Almighty," "Dear Lord and Father
of mankind," and "O Master, let me walk with Thee" illustrate
some of these principal moods.

During the bombings of World War II, Londoners huddled
in air raid cellars would express their calm faith by singing "Our
God, our Help in ages past." Parents and loved ones of military
men sing with unusual fervor whenever the hymn, "O God of
love, O King of peace, Make wars throughout the world to cease,"
is announced. Hymns express religious feelings.

2. *Through hymn singing, Christians proclaim their faith to others.* People are attracted by music because the love of tonal beauty is at the heart of all mankind. When noble texts are set to stirring melodies and are sung with real feeling, the effect is well-nigh irresistible. It is one of the most obvious ways of extending the Christian faith.

England was changed by one instance of this witnessing power of hymn singing. In 1736 John Wesley and his brother Charles, both ordained clergymen, were on board the little ship *Simmonds,* which was bound for Savannah, Georgia. Also aboard were twenty-six Moravian emigrants and their leader, Bishop David Nitschmann. At noon on Sunday, January 25, a frightful tempest struck the *Simmonds,* the fury of which increased in violence all afternoon. At seven that evening, John Wesley and other shipmates attended the vesper service of these German Christians. Wesley graphically describes the experience in his *Journal.*

> In the midst of the psalm wherewith their service began, wherein we were mentioning the power of God, the sea broke over, split the mainsail in pieces, covered the ship, and poured in between the decks, as if the great deep had already swallowed us up. A terrible screaming began among the English. The Germans looked up, and without intermission calmly sang on. I asked one of them afterwards, "Were you not afraid?" He answered, "I thank God, no." I asked, "But were not your women and children afraid?" He replied mildly, "No; our women and children are not afraid to die."[1]

This wonderful experience, wherein the Moravians witnessed to their calm faith by their singing, brought nearer to maturity the Wesleys' friendship with them and probably led directly to the brothers' later Aldersgate experience of conversion. From this experience they went out into the fruitful ministry which transformed the heart of England.

In less dramatic ways thousands of strangers have been influenced by hymn singing. Seekers after Christian truth and fellowship have been repelled by the refrigeration of atmosphere as men of ideas, leaders in industry, and prominent churchwomen stood mute and disinterested while the choir sang the hymns.

Conversely, many strangers have been irresistibly attracted to a particular congregation because the members very clearly had a vital faith and joyfully proclaimed it in song.

3. *Through hymn singing, Christians are bound in closer fellowship.* Some psychologists believe that collections of people remain individuals until a single event or purpose or emotion molds them into groups, and that then the group lives, feels, and thinks in a way of its own, superior in energy and intensity to the activity of any of its members. When a group of Christians sings with vitality the same melody, responds to identical rhythms, thinks and feels the same ideas and emotions during the act of common praise, it becomes well-nigh inevitable that each is drawn closer in spirit to his neighbor. They cease to be isolated individuals. They become indeed more completely members of the body of Christ.

As Christians, we are "elect from every nation, yet one o'er all the earth." But since it is so easy to feel our Christian fellowship with Chinese across the globe and so hard for some to acknowledge neighbors of another race as brethren in the faith, and since it is so easy to become ecclesiastical isolationists and religious nationalists, we need to use every means of grace in making real our unity with the brethren. Hymn singing is such a means.

"Dear Lord and Father of mankind" was written by the Quaker poet, Whittier. The British statesman, Sir John Bowring, a Unitarian, wrote "In the cross of Christ I glory." "I heard the voice of Jesus say" is by the Scotsman, Dr. Bonar, a Presbyterian. Frederick Faber, the London priest of Roman Catholicism, gave us "There's a wideness in God's mercy." Bishop Heber, of the Church of England, wrote "Holy, Holy, Holy! Lord God Almighty!" The Baptist country parson, John Fawcett, wrote "Blest be the tie that binds." Some unknown Negro first sang "Were you there when they crucified my Lord?" A Scotsman wrote "I bind my heart this tide" and a German wrote "Now thank we all our God." Sibelius, a Finn, composed the noble melody FINLANDIA, while a Russian, Bortniansky of Petrograd, composed the lovely VESPER HYMN. Surely a person who is aware of the diverse sources of these hymns and tunes cannot long sing them without feeling his at-one-ness with all the redeemed throughout the earth.

> One the strain that lips of thousands
> Lift as from the heart of one.[2]

A Christian should sense the continuity of Christian experience in all ages. He must be nerved by contact with ancient Christians who fought the good fight. Hymns make real this unseen fellowship with all the saints. Millions of Christians through four centuries have lifted to the skies the Reformation chorale "A mighty Fortress is our God." Probably the most familiar tune in Christendom is OLD HUNDREDTH, the Doxology tune, first announced four hundred years ago by John Calvin to the Geneva congregation. And, in the more distant past, the great Origen may have joined with his classmates around the feet of their renowned teacher, Clement of Alexandria, and heard him read to them his hymn "Shepherd of eager youth." Seventeen centuries ago! The deepest thoughts and experiences of these saints are ours through their hymns.

> O blest communion, fellowship divine!
> We feebly struggle, they in glory shine;
> Yet all are one in Thee, for all are Thine.
> Alleluia! Alleluia![3]

So the unifying power of hymns brings the individual Christian closer to the members of his immediate congregation; it helps him feel his brotherhood with Christians of varied creeds, nations, and races; and, finally, it leads him into the blessed fellowship with the redeemed of all ages.

4. *Through hymn singing, believers are taught Christian truth.* People absorb a great deal of Christian truth from the hymns which they sing. The great foundation doctrines of our faith are included in our hymnals. These truths, interpreted by godly men and women in simple and penetrating language, are easy to recall because of rhythmic cadence and recurrent rhyme. When borne on the wings of song, they can reach the inner spirits of worshipers.

For those who, in Paul's words, "sing with the understanding,"[4]

THE VALUES OF CONGREGATIONAL SINGING

there is laid out each week a table spread with spiritual nourishment. For example, one who sings with full comprehension, "The Church's one Foundation is Jesus Christ her Lord," will thereafter have a richer concept of the Church and its mission in the world today.

5. _Through hymn singing, Christians are sustained in daily life._ The truths contained in hymns, recalled in moments of trouble, undergird our lives. A person tossing upon a sleepless bed, tense and worried, can find soothing relief in the words of the fourth stanza of "Dear Lord and Father of mankind," which begins "Drop Thy still dews of quietness, till all our strivings cease." Paul and Silas in a Philippian jail felt assurance as they sang their songs in the night. Sir Wilfred Grenfell, snow-blind and nearly frozen, floating out to sea on an ice pan after his dog sled had plunged through the ice shelf, testified that he had no sense of fear, that he was sustained by the words of an old hymn which kept returning to his mind:

> My God and Father, while I stray
> Far from my home, on life's rough way,
> O teach me from my heart to say,
> "Thy will be done."[5]

3 What Is Superior Congregational Singing?

How can we know that we have good congregational singing? Some leaders think that the height of congregational singing has been attained when the largest possible volume of sound has issued from the throats of the people. If so, an electronic volume meter could determine which of two congregations will "outsing" the other.

John Wesley was too wise to accept such a shallow test for determining excellence of praise. In the *Minutes of Conference*, 1746, he instructed his early Methodist preachers to interrupt a noisy hymn and ask questions of the congregation: "Now do you know what you said last? Did it suit your case? Did you sing it as to God, with the spirit and understanding also?"

If the singing of a congregation meets the following four tests, the singing certainly could be considered superior.

1. The Congregation Sings with Understanding and Spirit

The Apostle Paul said, "I will sing with the spirit, and I will sing with the understanding also." (I Corinthians 14:15.) The thought and emotion contained in the text of a hymn must be understood and felt by each singer. The music is simply a vehicle for the joint expression of these ideas and feelings. John Wesley has this advice for singers who desire to sing with sincerity and intelligence:

> Above all, sing *spiritually*. Have an eye to God in every word you sing. Aim at pleasing *Him* more than yourself, or any other creature. In order to do this, attend strictly to

> the sense of what you sing, and see that your *Heart* is not
> carried away with the sound, but offered to God continually;
> so shall your singing be such as the Lord will approve of
> here, and reward you when He cometh in the clouds of
> heaven.[1]

2. *The Congregation Sings Musically*

Good congregational singing obeys such simple musical rules
as united attack, spirited movement at tempo set by the organist
or pianist, blended firm tone, and vital rhythm. As Sir Walford
Davies well said:

> Here we wish to endorse and emphasize the view that
> congregational singing will never even approach its best
> until a start is made on the principle that the fundamental
> principles of choralism should be aimed at in the nave no
> less than in the choir. Attack, unanimity, vital tone and
> rhythm: these call for no degree of skill beyond that attain-
> able by any normally intelligent crowd of adults.[2]

Wesley has forthright, practical advice for achieving this:

> Sing *lustily*, and with a good courage. Beware of singing
> as if you are half-dead or half-asleep; but lift up your voice
> with strength. Be no more afraid of your voice now, nor
> more ashamed of its being heard, than when you sing the
> songs of Satan.
> Sing *modestly*. Do not bawl, so as to be heard above or
> distinct from the rest of the congregation—that you may
> not destroy the harmony—but strive to unite your voices
> together so as to make one clear melodious sound.
> Sing *in time*. Whatever time is sung be sure to keep
> with it. Do not run before nor stay behind it; but attend
> close to the leading voices, and move therewith as exactly
> as you can; and take care not to sing *too slow*. This drawling
> way naturally steals on all who are lazy; and it is high time
> to drive it out from among us, and sing all our tunes just
> as quick as we did at first.

3. *All of the Congregation Sings*

"Let the people praise thee, O God; let all the people praise
thee."[3] All Christians assembled in worship, regardless of native
musical ability or vocal skill, should lift their hearts and voices

to the Throne of Grace. The aged Christian, the child, the business executive, the housewife—all should sing. Even those few who feel that they cannot carry a tune should at least open the hymnal and thoughtfully read the words of the hymn while others sing. As Wesley says:

> Sing *All*. See that you join with the congregation as frequently as you can. Let not a slight degree of weakness or weariness hinder you. If it is a cross to you, take it up, and you will find it a blessing.

4. *The Congregation Sings a Wide Variety of Good Hymns*

The congregation which can sing only a dozen or so old favorites acceptably can hardly be said to have the quality of singing found in another enterprising congregation which knows a hundred or more excellent hymns. A student acquainted only with the contemporary American novel can hardly be considered a well-rounded scholar of American and British literature. He has missed the inspired works of Shakespeare, Milton, and other great writers. Thus a congregation which wanders through a score of familiar songs, even though it rotates in an accomplished fashion, is missing the vast treasures of hymnody to be found in the pages of our good hymnals.

So we may say that great congregational singing is being achieved when the entire congregation sings a sizable number of good hymns with spiritual perception and musical artistry.

Part Two

THE HYMN

CHAPTER 4 *The Hymn:*
Text and Tune

Hymns have untold influence on the faith and experience of Christians. In the *Handbook to the Church Hymnary* we read, "The discovery was early made in the Christian era that popular religion is moulded largely by the ideas enshrined in its hymns."[1] And this relationship between hymns and religion is expressed in Dr. Routley's words: "a depressed standard of hymnody betokens a depressed spiritual state."[2]

Since there is an interchange of influence between congregational music and faith, it is imperative that leaders know what constitutes merit in a hymn. This is required because few of our hymnals have not made some concessions to mediocrity. It is almost inevitable that a committee, shaping a denominational hymnal, will react to the demands of congregations for hymns made sacred by long association. These hymns, less than perfect in craftsmanship, may have served a useful purpose. However, leaders who are interested in betterment of singing should know how to distinguish the chaff from the wheat and to explain their reasons for so doing.

Our analysis of hymns will be divided into three parts: The Hymn Text; The Music of Hymns; and The Matching of Text and Tune.

THE HYMN TEXT

The final arbiter of greatness in a hymn is the test of long, satisfactory use by the Church. In Dr. C. S. Phillips' words, "Time, on the whole, is a sound critic in hymnody as in other matters: those hymns survive that deserve to survive."[3] The Basic List of Hymns in the next chapter includes hundreds of hymns which have been used by many branches of Christendom for a number of centuries. The quality of a majority of these hymns is incontestible.

The subject matter of hymns is as wide as Christian faith and experience. It far exceeds the classic limitations placed upon it by St. Augustine, who stated that hymns were "songs with praise to God." "Without praise," he claims, "they are not hymns," and neither are they "if they praise aught beside God." Although adoration of Almighty God must always remain at the center of church music, hymn writers have given us hymns which enable us to obey the Apostle Paul's injunction to teach and admonish one another "in psalms and hymns and spiritual songs."[4] So we have hymns addressed to fellow Christians ("Rise up, O men of God") or to ourselves ("Awake, my soul, stretch every nerve"). Nowadays we have hymns which express personal and national penitence, joy in Christian fellowship, loyalty to Christ, the mission enterprise, hope of life everlasting, and many other aspects of godly living.

For our definition of a good hymn, let us take the description of Isaac Watts' hymns given by Dr. Millar Patrick:

> ... he [Watts] set for ever the example of what the congregational hymn should be. What made his own hymns so popular was their fidelity to Scripture, their consistent objectivity and freedom from introspection, and their exact suitability, in ideas and in the limpid clearness of their language, for giving voice to the religious thought and emotion of the average believer; these qualities make his best hymns perfect for the expression of a congregation's worship. He showed also that a good hymn for popular use should have a single theme, organic unity, boldness of attack in the opening line, and a definite progression of thought throughout to a marked and decisive climax. Also, it should be short. His hymns are brief, compact, direct, and telling. Reasons like these justified James Montgomery in saying that Watts was "the real founder of English hymnody."[5]

From this definition we shall select these four salient points for amplification: (1) Scriptural fidelity, (2) spiritual reality and wholesomeness, (3) simplicity and beauty, and (4) structural soundness.

1. Scriptural Fidelity

Christian hymns have their root in the Book of God's revelation —the Holy Bible. Their lines either convey almost verbatim the text of Scripture ("How firm a foundation, ye saints of the Lord" or " 'Twas on that night when doomed to know"), or contain a generous amount of explicit reference to the Bible ("Where cross the crowded ways of life") or simply express an experience or truth based on the contents of Holy Writ. This close correlation between hymnal and Bible is graphically shown in the indexes of Scriptural allusions which appear with increasing frequency in hymnals and hymnal handbooks.[6]

2. Spiritual Reality and Wholesomeness

The hymn must come from the heart of the writer if it is to move the heart of the singer. There must be an experience of spiritual reality at the source. John Drinkwater has written that "contact with fine poetry is precisely contact with most vital and personal experience conveyed to us in the most persuasive medium invented by man . . . pregnant and living words."[7]

To Martin Luther, God was a mighty Fortress. To him life was a struggle whose outcome was sure—"And He must win the battle . . . His Kingdom is forever." The object of this immortal hymn is to rouse our dormant faith and to nerve us with the spiritual energy and fortitude of the German Reformer.

One has only to read the following lines of the blind Scotsman, George Matheson, to catch the measure of devotion in his heart:

> Make me a captive, Lord,
> And then I shall be free;
> Force me to render up my sword,
> And I shall conquerer be.

> I sink in life's alarms
>   When by myself I stand;
> Imprison me within Thine arms,
>   And strong shall be my hand.

We must keenly scrutinize hymns in current use to determine whether they have positive values and wholesome influences. Evelyn Underhill's warning should be cited:

> . . . This tendency of the received suggestion to work out its whole content for good or evil within the unconscious mind, shows the importance which we ought to attach to the tone of a religious service, and how close too many of our popular hymns are to what one might call psychological sin; stressing as they do a childish weakness and love of shelter and petting, a neurotic shrinking from full human life, a morbid preoccupation with failure and guilt. Such hymns make devitalizing suggestions, adverse to the health and energy of the spiritual life; and are all the more powerful because they are sung collectively and in rhythm, and are cast in an emotional mould.[8]

3. Simplicity and Beauty

The act of hymn singing provides no opportunity for leisurely reflection on the text. Furthermore, congregations include many degrees of cultural and intellectual achievement. Hymn meanings must therefore be readily apparent. High-flown allusions, involved structure, or long, unfamiliar words reduce comprehension. If, with the Apostle Paul, we are to "sing with the understanding," the text must be immediately understandable.

In the original preface to Isaac Watts' hymns, he stated that he "endeavored to make the sense plain and obvious . . . I have cut out the lines that are too sonorous . . . lest a more exalted Turn of Thought or Language should darken or disturb the Devotion of the plainest Souls."[9]

This statement should not be construed to mean that the beauty of true poetry cannot be present in hymns. Indeed, the kindling of imagination through an exact turn of word can illumine the mind with an unforgettable spiritual truth. Read the following stanzas from two hymns of this century:

> Our God, to whom we turn
>   When weary with illusion,
> Whose stars serenely burn
>   Above this earth's confusion,
> Thine is the mighty plan,
>   The steadfast order sure,
> In which the world began,
>   Endures, and shall endure.[10]

> All beautiful the march of days,
>   As seasons come and go;
> The Hand that shaped the rose hath wrought
>   The crystal of the snow;
> Hath sent the hoary frost of heaven,
>   The flowing water sealed,
> And laid a silent loveliness
>   On hill and wood and field.[11]

4. Structural Soundness

Single theme, organic unity, boldness of attack in the opening line, definite progression of thought throughout to a marked and decisive climax, brevity—the presence of these qualities will give a hymn architectural soundness. These characteristics are exemplified in the better hymns of Isaac Watts and Charles Wesley.

There are many patterns which give organic unity to hymns.[12] Some are based on the Trinity, with stanzas devoted to the attributes of each Person of the Godhead ("Come, Thou Almighty King" and "Ancient of Days"). Another example is the hymn based on Jesus' words, "I am the way, the truth, and the life" ("Thou art the Way: to Thee alone").[13] An outstanding instance of a hymn organized to describe the characteristics of God is Henry Hallam Tweedy's "Eternal God, whose power upholds":

> Eternal God, whose power upholds
> Both flower and flaming star,
> To whom there is no here nor there,
> No time, no near nor far,

No alien race, no foreign shore,
No child unsought, unknown:
O send us forth, Thy prophets true,
To make all lands Thine own!

O God of love, whose spirit wakes
In every human breast,
Whom love, and love alone, can know,
In whom all hearts find rest:
Help us to spread Thy gracious reign
Till greed and hate shall cease,
And kindness dwell in human hearts,
And all the earth find peace!

O God of truth, whom science seeks
And reverent souls adore,
Who lightest every earnest mind
Of every clime and shore:
Dispel the gloom of error's night,
Of ignorance and fear,
Until true wisdom from above
Shall make life's pathway clear!

O God of beauty, oft revealed
In dreams of human art,
In speech that flows to melody,
In holiness of heart:
Teach us to ban all ugliness
That blinds our eyes to Thee,
Till all shall know the loveliness
Of lives made fair and free!

O God of righteousness and grace,
Seen in the Christ, Thy Son,
Whose life and death reveal Thy face,
By whom Thy will was done:

Inspire Thy heralds of good news
To live Thy life divine,
Till Christ is formed in all mankind
And every land is Thine![14]

These stanzas of Dr. Tweedy's not only manifest the theme of world-wide proclamation of the grace and love of God revealed in Christ, but they also exemplify the other structural qualities mentioned by Dr. Patrick in the definition quoted above. Note the magnificent opening which captures the imagination with the sweep of the control of the Omnipotent. Observe how the second, third, and fourth stanzas show what is meant when the God of love, truth, and beauty enters the human spirit. Then we have a telling final stanza of consecration to bring the hymn to a firm climax. Each stanza is organized about a facet of the major theme of the nature of God. (For another hymn of unusual worth based on the same pattern as Dr. Tweedy's, see "Our God, to whom we turn" by Edward Grubb, Presbyterian *Hymnbook* 128, Episcopal *Hymnal 1940* 283.)

THE MUSIC OF HYMNS

A hymn tune is a musical form of sufficient simplicity and appeal that it can be sung without rehearsal by a congregation of musical amateurs. Its total structure must be of such a nature as to interpret almost equally all stanzas of a hymn. Only rarely is a hymn text provided with a different musical support for various stanzas of differing moods. (See, for example, the unison and four-part versions of Dr. Vaughan Williams' tune SINE NOMINE, No. 126 in *The Hymnal 1940*.)

A hymn tune is a living organism as it is being sung, and its effects are complex. Simultaneously we are influenced by the shape of the melody, the particular chord, the duration of the tone, and the location within the phrase and entire melody. In analyzing the components of a good hymn tune, then, we can consider them under four headings: Melody, Harmony, Rhythm (time measurement), and Structure.

1. *Melody*

The range of a good hymn tune must obviously remain within the compass of the average churchgoer's voice. The octave D to D is kept as the usual limits by many hymnal editors. An occasional excursion to a high F (or E flat in some editions) as in CRUSADER's HYMN "Fairest Lord Jesus" is manageable. One finds tunes with very limited range such as HAMBURG "When I survey the wondrous cross," with a compass from E natural to B flat. On the other hand there are tunes with a range of a tenth, such as MONKLAND "Let us with a gladsome mind." The outside congregational range seems to be an interval of a twelfth as found in "The Star-Spangled Banner" and DRESDEN "We plough the fields."

While some choir altos and basses have complained because lower keys in hymns have thrust their choral lines too low for comfort, the fact remains that hymns are congregational rather than choral and therefore the abilities of the layman to maneuver the melody must remain the prime consideration.

The *tessitura* or general average pitch of the melody is also a factor in determining the key. I prefer the key of C for "A mighty Fortress is our God" rather than the key of D. By the same token I would lower the key of LASST UNS ERFREUEN "All creatures of our God and King" from the key of E flat to D or possibly D flat. I have observed and sympathized with the vocal strain experienced by some congregations singing all six stanzas of this hymn in the key of E flat.

Regarding the structure of the melody, the British Archbishops' Committee on Music in Worship said this:

> Steep, disjunct, irresponsible, lavish ups and downs seem unfitting in church melody. Higher value is set in church upon quiet things. Melody can depict both strength and grace, and among the factors to be taken into account these three may be specially noted: (1) advance by steps of a second; (2) euphony in the larger intervals; and (3) *arpeggio* movement through common chords. These three, in a gracious but vital blend, should never fail to produce a fitting church melody.[15]

There are scores, even hundreds, of melodies in the better hymnals which illustrate these basic principles. To mention just a few, study St. Peter "In Christ there is no East or West" (P 479), St. Columba "The King of love my Shepherd is" (P106, E345), Lyons and Hanover "O worship the King" (P26, E288), Darwall's 148th "Rejoice, the Lord is King" (P140; see E600), St. Anne "Our God, our Help in ages past" (P111, E289), and Old Hundredth "All people that on earth do dwell" (P24; see E277). These melodies are based on the diatonic (whole and half step) scales. It is generally agreed that this type of scale has more virility than one which is essentially chromatic.

One test of an adequate hymn melody is its impressiveness when sung unadorned by harmony. Unison singing is considered such a desideratum by some denominations that the pew edition is a melody-only edition (Episcopal *Hymnal* 1940). Most other denominations, nevertheless, provide the full music edition for the congregation in the realization that many musically literate laymen desire on suitable hymns to sing the parts. Those hymns adapted mainly for unison singing are so marked above the music score in the hymnal.

2. *Harmony*

The harmony is the tonal garb of the melody. The character of the melody is modified, sometimes completely altered, by the type of harmonization. There are three main types found in many hymnals.

(1) *Unison.* As we have just said, certain melodies are intrinsically adapted for unison singing only. In the following examples of unison tunes the harmonies are thickened or thinned instrumentally according to the needs of the moment: Slane (P303, E122); Sine Nomine (P425, E126); Purpose (P500, E538); Divinum Mysterium (P7, E20).

(2) *Light-textured harmonization.* An increasing use is being made of light-textured harmonization, especially for children's songs. The child's voice does not need, in many cases, the weight of accompaniment required by adult voices. Dr. Austin C. Lovelace reharmonized Onslow "Father, we thank Thee for the night" in this direction for the Presbyterian *Hymnbook* (No. 467). The beautiful traditional melody Covenanters (P153) has a remarkably skillful 3-part harmonization. The accompanist's edition of

Our Songs of Praise (Concordia) and *The Canyon Hymnal for Boys and Girls* (Canyon Press) are splendid models of this lighter harmonization for children's music.

(3) *Four-part harmonization.* The enormous majority of hymn tunes have harmony in four parts. While the soprano melody is the principal and identifying tune, ideally all other lines should have musical worth and individuality. In other words, a bass, tenor, or alto should find his or her vocal line as satisfying and challenging as the soprano line is to the soprano singers.

Fortunately our hymnals are supplied with an increasing list of well-harmonized melodies. Classic examples of superb craftsmanship, of course, are the polyphonic chorales of Johann Sebastian Bach (for example, PASSION CHORALE P194, E75; JESU, MEINE FREUDE P414, E453; and O GOTT, DU FROMMER GOTT P128). However, contemporary composers such as Geoffrey Shaw (STRACATHRO P327, E325), Joseph Parry (ABERYSTWYTH P216, E415), Hilton Rufty (BOUNDLESS MERCY P39), and Hugh Davies (ARFON P197) show unusual ability in weaving skillful harmonies. Contrast the vocal lines of any of these examples with the alto line of, say, the tune WATCHMAN "Watchman, tell us of the night" by Lowell Mason (E440), in which out of fifty-six notes the altos sing the same D on forty-eight of them. (Notice, however, the lovely folk-song quality which emerges in Dr. T. Tertius Noble's arrangement of this same tune on the opposite page of this hymnal.)

The harmonic palette of the musical artist is almost limitless. Within the limits of ecclesiastical dignity he can create a keen sense of interest and vitality by his choice of chords. Notice the dynamic thrust given to the second and fourth lines[16] of the stirring Irish traditional melody DURROW (P93), by the dissonant second chord:

Rev. J. B. Dykes in his familiar tune NICAEA could have har-
monized the first phrase of "Holy, Holy, Holy! Lord God Almighty" as follows, using only two chords:

As it is, Dykes used almost a dozen different chords in this brief
phrase:

When a section of the melodic line is repeated, the composer or
arranger frequently offers a different treatment the second time. In
the French hymn melody PICARDY, a three-measure phrase is har-
monized in the following two ways:

The editors of the Episcopal hymnal availed themselves of this opportunity in the tune Moscow ("Come, Thou Almighty King"; the tune is frequently called ITALIAN HYMN). Whereas most hymnals repeat the little melodic rise with identical chords, the Episcopal editors give this variation:

Observe also how the editors of the Episcopal hymnal varied this four-measure phrase in the familiar tune St. CATHERINE ("Faith of our fathers," E393):

Some hymn tune writers had a gift of melody but very limited technical equipment when it came to harmonization. Tonic, subdominant, and dominant chords were the main buttresses. Others were enamored of such devices as the seventh chord. In some hymnals, these harmonizations have been refurbished.

It is instructive to observe the care with which the musical editors of the Episcopal hymnal reworked certain familiar tunes. When a given harmonization of a popular hymn tune has become fastened in the affections of millions of Christians of many denominations, it behooves reforming editors to walk circumspectly when contemplating changes of harmony. If a tune has always appeared in public in gingham, it is something of a shock to watch it issue forth in sable and silks (to say nothing of the ire bred in the minds of bass singers who memorized the former bass line thirty years earlier).

To be specific, the reharmonization of MARTYN ("Jesus, Lover of my soul," E415) is adroit and very successful. Whereas most editors have accepted the harmonic status quo and kept the deadening reiteration of the tonic chord at the end of each phrase, the Episcopal musicians have moved the final chord of the third line to the welcome dominant. They have introduced occasional inversions, passing notes, minors, dissonants, and yet have kept the plain character of the original so that the average layman hardly knows that anything different has been happening except, probably, that his interest in the text has somehow been maintained more than usual. Notice these phrases:

These editors have also done a fine job of pruning seventh chords from the tune GALILEE ("Jesus calls us," E566). Although a few are necessarily left for legitimate transition chords, there are seven fewer chords of this type than in most hymnals.

An exquisite job of reharmonization is seen in Canon Winfred Douglas' work on the tune LUKE (or SWEET STORY) "I think when I read that sweet story of old" (P460, E246). Play first the old Bradbury harmonization found in many hymnals, then the Douglas, and notice the contrast.

These illustrations will show some of the effects which harmony can have on melody.

3. Rhythm (Time Measurement)

The basic patterns of time are important factors in the effect of a hymn tune. This temporal behavior determines to a great extent the mood created by the hymn. The writers of the Archbishops' report on church music had this to say:

> Music may move quietly, may leap, or even dance. Clearly its movement or rhythm must be seemly. Church-rhythms should certainly be full of life; but they should as certainly have the needed dignity without heaviness; strength and a pervasive enthusiasm without levity. In short, such rhythms should manifest joyous reticence. . . . It may be noticed that nursery rhymes have for their rhythmic characteristic the constant iteration of some little snippet or pattern of longs and shorts. This is named here as being the extreme opposite of that which is needed in church-rhythms. They should never degenerate into small-minded rhythmic figures, pirouetting round a point. They should move forward towards their goal, as it were on pilgrimage.[17]

The subject of rhythm as applied to the playing and interpretation of hymns is discussed in some detail in chapter 9. Suffice it to say now that hundreds of tunes in top hymnals exhibit the variety of rhythmic structures which support and give vitality to the melodies to which they are wedded. These patterns can be best analyzed by dissociating them from the melody and seeing them as temporal units only. Try this with such tunes as NICAEA "Holy, Holy, Holy! Lord God Almighty," LOBE DEN HERREN "Praise ye the Lord, the Almighty, the King of creation," and OLD 124TH "Turn back, O man." One advantage of patterns such as these is the nearly equal emphasis given to each syllable of the text. Indeed, some of our tunes have only time units of equal length. See TALLIS' CANON, as a sample.

At the opposite pole are the flippant, rhythmically jerky snatches of melody sung by some church groups. When such tunes are attached to sacred words, we are reminded of Dr. Louis Benson's complaint:

This gift of inattention, so far as hymnody is concerned, has been greatly fostered, no doubt, by the quick and rattling melodies and the rapid verse which the young people are trained to sing. In the meantime the teaching power of great hymns remains, an asset of the Church hardly included in the inventory of her educational resources, and in her educational practice generally disregarded.[18]

An instructive study in the effect of duration on melody may be made by playing the "ironed out" version of OLD HUNDREDTH (as sung with the Doxology by many congregations) after one has played the original as developed in Geneva by Louis Bourgeois (see P544 for former and P24 for latter). For similar effect try playing the tune EVENTIDE "Abide with me" with equal time values for each chord!

4. *Structure*

Even within its brief compass, a well-structured hymn tune will manifest the unity and variety of true art. Dr. Routley singles out HANOVER as one of the best.[19] Each of its phrases will be shaped so that the tones lead inevitably to the climax of the phrase, which is frequently the highest and/or longest note. And, just as important, the phrases must be so masterfully juxtaposed that the singers are led through lesser curves of energy to the central apex of the composition and then back to the repose of the final tone. An analysis of the tune LYONS "O worship the King" (P26) is a rewarding study in tune architecture.

Within the structure of a popular hymn tune we find a variety of thematic repetitions. In the most familiar of Christmas carols "Silent Night" we find three brief bits of melody, each repeated twice, which constitute a major portion of the total tune. Here are some other examples of thematic patterns:

AABA	EBENEZER (P361, E519), FOREST GREEN (P256, E21)
ABB	MORNING SONG (P508, E156)
AB¹AB²	HAMBURG (P198, E219)
AABBCCBBBBB	LASST UNS ERFREUEN (P33), VIGILES ET SANCTI (E599)

THE MATCHING OF TEXT AND TUNE

Words and music combine to convey the spiritual import of
the hymn to the mind and heart of the Christian. Like a successful marriage of man and woman, the finest hymns are those which
have a magnificent text and a strong, beautiful tune. Martin
Luther and Georg Neumark each gave to Christianity a hymn
which exemplifies fully this successful combining of words and
music. Each composed both the text and the tune. The hymns
are "A mighty Fortress is our God" (P91, E551) and "If thou
but suffer God to guide thee" (P344).

There are numerous instances where a strong hymn text has
survived even though wedded for years to a weaker tune. Usually,
but not always, these can be spotted in a hymnal by the presence
of an alternate tune. As a rule the better tune—in the opinion
of the editors—is given first, with the familiar but less desirable
melody given second. This is done in the hope that congregations
can gradually be weaned to the preferred tune. Of course there
are exceptions, such as the two superb melodies for "Fairest Lord
Jesus"—SCHÖNSTER HERR JESU and CRUSADER's HYMN. Sometimes,
in search of a better musical setting, the editors have found a
tune which was composed years ago. When one seems unavail-
able, then the committee may commission a new one. This was
done in the case of SINE NOMINE, composed by Dr. Ralph
Vaughan Williams for the *English Hymnal* (1906) to accompany
"For all the saints." Dr. Austin Lovelace supplied the well-
shaped tune HINMAN for the ancient text "Shepherd of eager
youth" (P471).

The major considerations in determining compatibility of text
and tune are metrical and emotional identity.

Identity of meter. It goes without saying that the metrical patterns of text and music such as Short Meter and 7.6.7.6.D. must be
the same. This is discussed in some detail in the section on the
indexes of the hymnal (chapter 7).

In this connection, we should mention that ideally the accents
of the words from stanza to stanza should fall in the same place.

As an illustration observe how Henry van Dyke in "Joyful, joyful, we adore Thee" was able to align the accented syllables. This means that the primary and secondary accents of the 4/4 tune HYMN TO JOY coincide with the accented syllables of the words, thus emphasizing the speech rhythm:

1.	Joy	-	ful,	joy	-	ful,	we	a	-	dore	Thee,
2.	All		Thy	works		with	joy	sur	-	round	Thee,
3.	Thou		art	giv	-	ing	and	for	-	giv	- ing,
4.	Mor	-	tals,	join		the	hap	-	py	cho	- rus.[20]

Most of the Watts and Wesley hymns also exhibit this consistency of accents from stanza to stanza.

Contrast this with the beginning of the third phrases of the eight stanzas in "For all the saints."

1.	Thy	name,	O	Je	-	sus,	be	for	-	ev	-	er	blest.
2.		Thou,	in the	dark	-	ness	drear,	their		one		true	Light.
3.	And	win	with	them		the	vic	-	tor's	crown		of	gold.
4.	Yet	all	are	one		in	Thee,	for		all		are	Thine.
5.	And	hearts	are	brave	a	-	gain,	and		arms		are	strong.
6.		Sweet	is the	calm		of	par	-	a	-	dise	the	blest.
7.	The	King	of	glo	-	ry	pass	-	es		on	His	way.
8.		Sing	- ing to	Fa	-	ther,	Son,	and		Ho	-	ly	Ghost,

This disparity of stanza accents (found to a degree in most hymns but exceptionally illustrated in this particular one) can either be forced into the stiff accentual pattern of a hymn tune (SARUM) or else an especially elastic tune can be shaped to fit the shifting stresses, as is shown in the magnificent tune SINE NOMINE by Dr. Ralph Vaughan Williams (P425, E126). For another illustration of this problem, see Martin Shaw's tune PURPOSE "God is working His purpose out" (P500, E538).

Having observed congregations stumble at these points of disparity or neglect to slip in two syllables where the preceding stanza had only one, the writer is inclined to agree with Robert Bridges, former poet laureate of England, who was discussing with a friend "whether the accented notes in the tune required always a corresponding accent in the words." He wrote as follows:

> I think that the intelligent hymn-singer is getting much too squeamish on this head. I do not find that an occasional disagreement between accent of words and of music offends me in a hymn. A fine tune is an unalterable artistic form, which pleases in itself and for itself. The notion of its giving way to the words is impossible. The words are better suited

if they fit in with *all* the quantities and accents of the tune, but it is almost impossible and not necessary that they should. Their *mood* is what the tune must be true to; and the mood is the main thing. If the tune also incidentally reinforces important words or phrases, that is all the better, and where there are refrains, or repetitions of words, the tune should be designed for them; but the enormous power that the tune has of enforcing or even of creating a mood is the one invaluable thing of magnitude, which overrules every other consideration.[21]

This is not to say that Vaughan Williams' tune SINE NOMINE is not a great hymn melody, but it is to urge that poets writing hymns should strive in so far as is possible toward regularity of accent from stanza to stanza.

Comprehension of the text is also furthered by the completion of a unit of thought within a single phrase or clause. Thus the musical and textual units coincide. To be specific, the congregation should not too often have to take a breath between the verb and its direct object. Here again we find models of conciseness in the hymns of Wesley and Watts.

Identity of emotion. As Robert Bridges states, there is an emotional tone to both text and tune and these should be mutually reinforcing. A poem extolling the greatness of our God and His creation must have music of nobility and loftiness. In the words of Dr. Benson:

> The hymn and its tune together compose the unit of the hymn as sung, and together stand or fall. An inartistic tune will kill the most poetic hymn ever written. A dull or unwelcome tune will impart to the most spiritual words an atmosphere of insincerity that makes one's spirit shrink. A tune adequate to the spiritual values of the words interprets them. A great tune does more: it adds something to the printed words by way of suggesting things of the spirit unprinted between the lines.[22]

CHAPTER 5 *Basic Hymns*
Arranged Chronologically

When Dr. John Julian finished his monumental *Dictionary of Hymnology* in 1892, he estimated that over 400,000 Christian hymns had been written by that time. By the present time the number probably far exceeds a half-million. Many of these, of course, are inferior and transitory, but thousands of them are splendid hymns. Denominational editorial committees have to winnow this mass of hymnody and settle usually upon approximately 600 hymns for the average-sized hymnbook. It need not be pointed out that each denominational choice varies according to its tradition and standards. Lutherans, for example, always include an ample portion of German chorales.

On the local church level a further selective process is performed by the minister and organist. Few congregations in the course of a year sing more than 100-150 different hymns. Naturally the repertoire of well-known hymns varies from congregation to congregation, depending considerably upon the favorite hymns of present and former local leadership.

What are the most important hymns in the hymnal? Since we can hardly expect the ordinary congregation to sing 600 different hymns, is there a nucleus with which an enterprising church leader can begin?

In compiling this list, an objective basis for selecting 120 hymns has been used. The remaining hymns are a personal selection. Here is how the list was compiled.

The following American and British hymnals were compared

to see what hymns were in all ten books and, next, what hymns were in at least nine of the ten hymnals.

The Hymn Book, 1938 (Anglican, Canada); *Christian Worship,* 1941 (Baptist-Disciples); *The Pilgrim Hymnal,* 1935 (Congregational Christian); *The Hymnal,* 1940 (Episcopal, U. S.); *Common Service Book,* 1918 (United Lutheran); *The Methodist Hymnal,* 1932 (Methodist); *The New Church Hymnal,* 1937 (undenominational); *The Hymnal,* 1933 (Presbyterian, USA); *Songs of Praise,* 1931 (Anglican, English); *The Hymnary,* 1930 (United Church of Canada).

Sixty-two hymns were in all ten hymnals. An additional 58 hymns were in nine of the ten books. This list of 120 hymns constitutes a remarkable ecumenical hymnody. In this body of widely sung hymns we will find most of the great hymns of the English language.[1]

To this list of 120 hymns have been added those which give historical and topical completion and are worthy of use. Other writers naturally would differ in their selection.

These hymns have been organized on a chronological basis.[2] Many worshipers have little idea of the significant religious movements which produced certain hymns. Therefore, the hymns have been grouped under seventeen headings, with a brief descriptive paragraph to summarize the historical period. In a book of this nature, there is no space for an extended historical treatment. Some excellent histories of hymnody are listed in the Bibliography at the end of the volume. Especially recommended is *The Story of the Church's Song* by Millar Patrick.

In order to make this listing more specific, the hymns under each chapter heading are listed in three alphabetical groups. The first group contains the hymns which appeared in all ten hymnals mentioned above. The second group contains those found in nine of the ten books cited, while additional selections will indicate hymns chosen by the writer. Along with each hymn title is shown the author of the text, and the date of authorship or publication. Next follows the tune name. Since all of these hymns may be consulted in either *The Hymnbook* (Presbyterian, 1955) or *The Hymnal* 1940 (Episcopal), the page numbers in these hymnbooks have been added after each title, the letter P and the letter E representing these two books respectively.

This list, then, will have a double purpose. It not only will give leaders an idea of the basic hymns sung by tens of millions of English-speaking Protestant Christians, but also it will at least suggest the historical context of each hymn. It is hoped that local church leaders will do these two things: (1) make a serious effort to learn and appreciate any unfamiliar hymns listed, and (2) gradually and skillfully introduce all of these hymns to the congregation.

1. The Church's First Heritage of Song: The Psalms

The ancient Hebrews in their tabernacle and temple worship made extensive use of singing and of musical instruments. The texts of many of their familiar songs are found in the Book of Psalms. These inspired utterances have been read, chanted, and sung by Christians for more than nineteen centuries. The Venite ("O come, let us sing unto the Lord," from Psalms 95 and 96; P586, E607-610) and the Jubilate ("O be joyful in the Lord," Psalm 100; P593, E642-646) are excellent samples of several psalms chanted by thousands of Christians each Sunday. Examples of metrical psalms are scattered through the following sections of this chapter, especially sections 6 and 8.

2. Hymns of the New Testament

Early fragmentary references lead us to believe that the wonderful vitality of the new Christian faith expressed itself in an outburst of song. Our Lord in the upper room hallowed for all time the use of singing by joining His disciples in a hymn before they went out into the Garden of Gethsemane. Paul urged the Ephesians and Colossians to teach and admonish one another with psalms and hymns and spiritual songs. The canticles found in Luke 1-2 (Magnificat, "My soul doth magnify the Lord," P596, E647-658; Benedictus, "Blessed be the Lord God of Israel," P592, E634-641; and Nunc Dimittis, "Lord, now lettest Thou Thy servant depart in peace," P597, E667-673) are still chanted in countless Christian congregations.

Although there are believed to be fragments of early Christian hymns embedded in the Epistles, these hymns seem not to have survived in their entirety. Here are two examples:

> Awake, O sleeper, and arise from the dead,
> and Christ shall give you light.
>> —Ephesians 5:14, R.S.V.

> He was manifested in the flesh,
> vindicated in the Spirit,
>> seen by angels,
> preached among the nations,
> believed on in the world,
>> taken up in glory.
>> —1 Timothy 3:16, R.S.V.

3. Greek Hymnody

During the first few centuries of the Christian era, Greek-speaking converts around the eastern Mediterranean penned some immortal hymns. These texts, frequently rising from bitter persecution and fierce doctrinal struggles, are loved and sung even to this day.

IN THE TEN HYMNALS CITED

The day of resurrection! John of Damascus, 8th century. LANCASHIRE. P208, E96.

IN NINE OF THE HYMNALS

Art thou weary, art thou languid. Suggested by writings of Stephen of Marsaba, 6th century. STEPHANOS. P264, E406.
Come, ye faithful. John of Damascus, 8th century. ST. KEVIN. P205, E94.

ADDITIONAL SELECTIONS

Christian, dost thou see them. Andrew of Crete, 8th century. ST. ANDREW OF CRETE. P360, E556.
Gloria in Excelsis (Glory be to God on high). c. 300. Old Scottish Chant. P572, E739.

Lord Jesus, think on me. Synesius of Cyrene, 4th century. SOUTH-
WELL, P270; ST. BRIDE, E417.

O gladsome light, O grace. Anon., 3rd century or earlier. NUNC
DIMITTIS. P61, E176.

Sanctus (Holy, holy, holy, Lord God of Hosts). P581-584, E735-
737.

Shepherd of eager youth. Clement of Alexandria, 2nd century.
HINMAN, P471. (Master of eager youth. MONK'S GATE, E362.)

Te Deum Laudamus (We praise Thee). Anon., 4th century. P589,
E613-622.

4. Latin Hymnody

In the fourth century, Augustine heard the singing of the Christians in Milan and wrote his impressions in the tenth book of his
Confessions:

> . . . when I remember the tears I shed at the Psalmody of
> Thy Church, in the beginning of my recovered faith; and
> how at this time I am moved, not with the singing, but
> with the things sung, when they are sung with a clear voice
> and modulation most suitable, I acknowledge the great use
> of this institution.[3]

During the 1,000 years of the Middle Ages (c.400-1400) an extensive hymnody flowed from the Latin Church. A lowly monk
in his stone cell, a wandering friar in central Italy, the influential
abbot of a large monastery—such men penned the following
hymns:

IN THE TEN HYMNALS CITED

All glory, laud, and honor. Theodulph of Orleans, c. 820. ST.
THEODULPH. P187, E62.

Jerusalem the golden. Bernard of Cluny, 12th century. EWING.
P428, E597.

Jesus, the very thought of Thee. Often attributed to Bernard of
Clairvaux, 12th century. ST. AGNES. P401, E462.

Jesus, Thou Joy of loving hearts. Often attributed to Bernard of
Clairvaux, 12th century. QUEBEC, P215; ABENDS, E485.

O come, O come, Emmanuel. Anon., 12th century. VENI EM-
MANUEL. P147, E2.
O sacred Head, now wounded. Ascribed to Bernard of Clairvaux,
12th century. PASSION CHORALE. P194, E75.

"Welcome, happy morning!" Venantius Fortunatus, 6th century.
FORTUNATUS. P207, E87.

ADDITIONAL SELECTIONS

All creatures of our God and King. Francis of Assisi, 1225. LASST
UNS ERFREUEN, P100. (Most High, omnipotent, good Lord.
ASSISI, E307.)
Christ is made the sure Foundation. Anon., 7th century. REGENT
SQUARE. P433, E384.
Christ is the world's Redeemer. Columba (521-597). MOVILLE.
P136.
Come, Holy Ghost, our souls inspire. Anon., c. 9th century. VENI
CREATOR. P237, E217.
Father, we praise Thee, now the night is over. Gregory I (540-
604). CHRISTE SANCTORUM. P43, E157.
Good Christian men, rejoice. Ascribed to Heinrich Suso, 14th cen-
tury. IN DULCI JUBILO. P165, E31.
Jesus Christ is risen today. Anon., 14th century. EASTER HYMN.
P204, E85.
Of the Father's love begotten. Aurelius Prudentius (348-413).
DIVINUM MYSTERIUM. P7, E20.
O God, Thou art the Father. Columba (521-597). DURROW. P93.
O Splendor of God's glory bright. Ambrose of Milan (340-397).
PUER NOBIS NASCITUR. P46, E158.
O what their joy and their glory must be. Abélard (1079-1142).
O QUANTA QUALIA. P424, E589.

5. The Hymnody of Germany

The Protestant Reformation restored congregational singing
after a silence of almost 1,200 years. The great reformer Luther
loved music and wrote some of our finest hymns. Luther wrote to

his friend Spalatin the following: "What I wish is to make German hymns for the people, that the Word of God may dwell in their hearts by means of song also." Luther and his followers and other German Christians for several centuries thereafter created the following hymns and chorales:

IN THE TEN HYMNALS CITED

A mighty Fortress is our God. Luther, 1529. EIN' FESTE BURG. P91, E551.

Now thank we all our God. Rinkart, c. 1636. NUN DANKET. P9, E276.

Praise ye the Lord, the Almighty. Neander, 1680. LOBE DEN HERREN. P1, E279.

The strife is o'er. Anon., c. 1695. VICTORY. P203, E91.

We plow the fields. Claudius, 1782. DRESDEN. P524, E138.

When morning gilds the skies. Anon., c. 1800. LAUDES DOMINI. P41, E367.

IN NINE OF THE HYMNALS

All my heart this night rejoices. Gerhardt, 1653. EBELING (BONN). P172, E32.

Give to the winds thy fears. Gerhardt, 1656. ST. BRIDE. P364.

My God, I love Thee; not because. Anon., 17th century. ST. FULBERT. E456.

Silent night! holy night! Mohr, 1818. STILLE NACHT. P154, E33.

Through the night of doubt and sorrow. Ingemann (Danish), 1825. ST. ASAPH. P475, E394.

ADDITIONAL SELECTIONS

Ah, dearest Jesus, holy Child. Luther, 1535. VON HIMMEL HOCH. P173, E23.

Be still, my soul. Schlegel, 1752. FINLANDIA. P374.

Fairest Lord Jesus. Anon., 17th century. SCHÖNSTER HERR JESU. P135, E346.

If thou but suffer God to guide thee. Georg Neumark, 1657. NEUMARK. P344.

Jesus, lead the way. Zinzendorf, 1721. SEELENBRÄUTIGAM (RO-CHELLE). P334, E425.

Jesus, priceless treasure. Franck, 1653. JESU, MEINE FREUDE. P414, E453.

Now woods and wolds are sleeping. Gerhardt, 1648. INNSBRUCK. P66. (The duteous day now closeth, E181.)

O Morning Star, how fair and bright. Nicolai, 1599. FRANKFORT. P415. (How bright appears the Morning Star, E329.)

Wake, awake, for night is flying. Nicolai, 1597. SLEEPERS, WAKE. E3.

6. Metrical Psalmody

After surveying the situation in Geneva, John Calvin drew up his "Essentials of a well-ordered Church," giving prominence to the psalms "we desire to be sung in church," for these three reasons: (1) The example of the ancient Church and St. Paul's testimony; (2) the warmth and uplift they would bring to our prayers, now so cold; (3) the discovery of what benefit and consolation the pope and his partisans have deprived the Church, by appropriating the psalms to be mumbled between them without understanding.[4]

John Calvin felt that he could find nothing better to sing than the 150 Psalms of David. Therefore these psalms, cast into metrical form, were sung by Calvin's followers in Switzerland, France, Britain, and elsewhere, frequently to the exclusion of hymns.

IN NINE OF THE HYMNALS

As pants the hart (Ps. 42). Tate and Brady, 1696. SPOHR, P322; MARTYRDOM, E450.

Let us with a gladsome mind (Ps. 136). Milton, 1623. MONKLAND. P28, E308.

ADDITIONAL SELECTIONS

All people that on earth do dwell (Ps. 100). Kethe, 1561. OLD HUNDREDTH. P24, E278.

I greet Thee, who my sure Redeemer art. John Calvin, 1545. TOULON. P144. (Although this is not a metrical psalm, it is included here because it was written by the founder of the Reformed tradition of psalm singing.)

My soul with expectation (Ps. 62). From *Scottish Psalter* of 1650. St. Flavian. P113.

Now Israel may say, and that in truth (Ps. 124). From *The Psalter* of 1912. Old 124th. P357.

O Lord, my God, most earnestly (Ps. 63). From *The Psalter* of 1912. Stracathro. P327.

O sing a new song to the Lord (Ps. 96). From *Scottish Psalter* of 1650. Song 67. P37.

The Lord's my Shepherd (Ps. 23). From *Scottish Psalter* of 1650. Crimond. P104.

7. *The Gathering Stream of British Hymnody*

Although many British congregations from the time of the Reformation (early 16th century) until the time of Isaac Watts (early 18th century) sang only metrical Old Testament psalms, there were during this period hymn writers who wanted to express their devotion in New Testament thought. So for many years in the British Isles these isolated streams of lyric expression had been gathering.

IN THE TEN HYMNALS CITED

All praise to Thee, my God. Ken, 1692, 1709. Tallis' Canon. P63, E165.

While shepherds watched their flocks. Tate, 1700. Christmas, P169; Winchester Old, E13.

IN NINE OF THE HYMNALS

The first Noel. Anon., c. 17th century. The First Noel. P156, E30.

The spacious firmament on high. Addison, 1712. Creation. P97, E309.

ADDITIONAL SELECTIONS

Awake, my soul, and with the sun. Ken, 1695. Morning Hymn. P50, E151.

Be Thou my Vision. Anon., Ancient Irish. SLANE. P303.

He who would valiant be. Bunyan, 1684. ST. DUNSTAN'S. P345, E563.

Let all the world in every corner sing. Herbert, 1633. HIGH ROAD. P22, E290.

When all Thy mercies, O my God. Addison, 1712. TALLIS' ORDINAL. P119, E297.

8. Watts' Psalms and Hymns

Isaac Watts (1674-1748), frequently called the "Father of English Hymnody," is generally credited with being mainly responsible for loosening the exclusive hold of metrical psalms in the English Church. His great hymns such as "When I survey the wondrous cross" and his Christianized psalms such as "Jesus shall reign" (Psalm 72) speeded the emancipation. His essays on the need for renovation of psalmody also paved the way.

IN THE TEN HYMNALS CITED

From all that dwell below the skies (Ps. 117). Watts, 1719. LASST UNS ERFREUEN, P33; OLD HUNDREDTH, E277.

Jesus shall reign where'er the sun (Ps. 72). Watts, 1719. DUKE STREET. P496, E542.

O God, our Help in ages past (Ps. 90). Watts, 1719. ST. ANNE. P111, E289.

When I survey the wondrous cross. Watts, 1707. HAMBURG, P198; ROCKINGHAM, E337.

IN NINE OF THE HYMNALS

Joy to the world! (Ps. 98). Watts, 1719. ANTIOCH, P161; RICHMOND, E319.

ADDITIONAL SELECTIONS

Alas! and did my Saviour bleed. Watts, 1707. MARTYRDOM (AVON). P199.

Before Jehovah's awful throne (Ps. 100). Watts, 1705, 1719. PARK STREET. P81. (Before the Lord Jehovah's throne. WINCHESTER NEW, E300.)

Come, we that love the Lord. Watts, 1709. St. Thomas. P408.
Lord of the worlds above (Ps. 84). Watts, 1719. Darwall's 148th. P14.
This is the day the Lord hath made (Ps. 118). Watts, 1719. Arlington. P69.

9. The Hymns of the Wesleys

The Wesley brothers, John (1703-1791) and Charles (1707-1788), went the length and breadth of Britain preaching and singing the Gospel of Christ. In this Great Awakening, Charles was the hymn writer, composing over 6,500 hymns. He brought into existence two new kinds of hymns, the hymn of Christian experience and the evangelistic hymn. John translated some fine German texts (see "Give to the winds thy fears"). Together they edited many hymnals. Both men were keenly aware of the need for an educational approach to evangelistic music. For this reason their revival music has lasted and has met the tests of centuries.

IN THE TEN HYMNALS CITED

Hark, the herald angels sing. C. Wesley, 1739. Mendelssohn. P163, E27.
Jesus, Lover of my soul. C. Wesley, 1740. Aberystwyth and Martyn. P216, E415.
Love divine, all loves excelling. C. Wesley, 1747. Beecher, P399; Hyfrydol, E479.

IN NINE OF THE HYMNALS

Christ the Lord is risen today. C. Wesley, 1739. Nassau, E95. (Easter Hymn is the tune used in many hymnals.)
Christ, whose glory fills the skies. C. Wesley, 1740. Lux Prima, P47; Ratisbon, E153.
O for a thousand tongues to sing. C. Wesley, 1739. Azmon, P141; Stracathro, E325.
Soldiers of Christ, arise. C. Wesley, 1749. Diademata, P362; Silver Street, E552.

ADDITIONAL SELECTIONS

A charge to keep I have. C. Wesley, 1762. BOYLSTON. P301.

Come, Thou long-expected Jesus. C. Wesley, 1744. HYFRYDOL or
STUTTGART. P151, E1.

Rejoice, the Lord is King. C. Wesley, 1746. DARWALL'S 148TH,
P140; JUBILATE, E350.

Ye servants of God, your Master proclaim. C. Wesley, 1744.
HANOVER. P27.

10. Eighteenth-Century British Hymnody

In addition to the outstanding works of Watts and the Wesleys,
the eighteenth century produced countless other hymn writers,
notably the two Calvinists, Cowper and Newton, who in 1779
issued a collection called "Olney Hymns." The winnowing process
of the years has left us the following choice hymns:

IN THE TEN HYMNALS CITED

All hail the power of Jesus' name! Perronet, 1779, 1780. COR-
ONATION. P132, E355.

Glorious things of thee are spoken. Newton, 1779. AUSTRIAN
HYMN. P434, E385.

God moves in a mysterious way. Cowper, 1774. DUNDEE (FRENCH).
P112, E310.

How sweet the name of Jesus sounds. Newton, 1779. ST. PETER.
P130, E455.

O come, all ye faithful. Anon., 18th century. ADESTE FIDELES. P170,
E12.

Rock of Ages. Augustus M. Toplady, 1776. TOPLADY. P271, E471.

IN NINE OF THE HYMNALS

Children of the Heavenly King. Cennick, 1742. PLEYEL'S HYMN.
P340, E578.

Guide me, O Thou great Jehovah. Williams, 1745. CWM
RHONDDA, P339; ST. OSWALD, E434.

How firm a foundation. Anon. (K), 1787. FOUNDATION, P369;
LYONS, E564.

Lord, dismiss us with Thy blessing. Fawcett, 1773. SICILIAN
MARINERS. P79, E489.

O for a closer walk with God. Cowper, 1769. DALEHURST or
BEATITUDO. P319, E416.

O God of Bethel, by whose hand. Doddridge, 1736. DUNDEE
(FRENCH). P342, E497.

Praise the Lord: ye heavens, adore Him. Anon., 1796. FABEN. P3.

ADDITIONAL SELECTIONS

Amazing grace—how sweet the sound. Newton, 1779. AMAZING
GRACE. P275.

Awake, my soul, stretch every nerve. Doddridge, 1755. CHRISTMAS.
P346, E577.

Come, Thou Almighty King. Anon., c. 1757. ITALIAN HYMN
(Moscow). P244, E271.

Hark, my soul, it is the Lord! Cowper, 1768. ST. BEES, P263;
CAMPION, E459.

Lo! He comes, with clouds descending. Cennick, 1752. HOLYWOOD
(ST. THOMAS). P234, E5.

There is a fountain filled with blood. Cowper, 1771. CLEANSING
FOUNTAIN. P276.

11. Nineteenth-Century British Hymnody: The Romantic Literary Movement

The early nineteenth century witnessed a renascence of wonder,
which in the literary world expressed itself in renewed interest in
the world of nature (for example, the poems of Wordsworth). It
included also a romantic review of ancient culture and history
(for example, the novels of Walter Scott). It affected hymnody by
stimulating interest in beauty of literary expression as well as in
depth of religious feeling. Bishop Reginald Heber best exemplifies
this period.

IN THE TEN HYMNALS CITED

Bread of the world in mercy broken. Heber, 1827. EUCHARISTIC
HYMN. P445, E196.

Brightest and best of the sons of the morning. Heber, 1811. MORNING STAR. P175, E46.

God, that madest earth and heaven. Heber, 1827. AR HYD Y NOS. P58, E169.

Holy, Holy, Holy! Lord God Almighty! Heber, 1826. NICAEA. P11, E266.

Ride on! ride on in majesty! Milman, 1827. ST. DROSTANE. P188, E64.

The Son of God goes forth to war. Heber, 1827. ALL SAINTS NEW. P354, E549.

IN NINE OF THE HYMNALS

Strong Son of God, immortal Love. Tennyson, 1850. ST. CRISPIN, P228; PALISADES, E365.

12. Nineteenth-Century British Hymnody: The Oxford Movement

Not to be confused with the recent Oxford Group Movement, the nineteenth-century Oxford Movement was an effort, centering in Oxford, England, in the 1830's, to revitalize the Church of England. It owed its start to a memorable sermon on "National Apostasy," preached by the brilliant John Keble. In the world of hymnody this movement not only produced the following hymns but it also led to the rediscovery and translation of many of the ancient Latin and Greek hymns listed earlier. John Mason Neale and Edward Caswall were two skilled translators.

IN THE TEN HYMNALS CITED

Sun of my soul. Keble, 1820. HURSLEY. P56, E166.

There's a wideness in God's mercy. Faber, 1854. IN BABILONE, P110; BEECHER, E304.

IN NINE OF THE HYMNALS

Lead, kindly Light. Newman, 1833. LUX BENIGNA. P331, E430.

New every morning is the love. Keble, 1822. MELCOMBE. P45, E155.

ADDITIONAL SELECTIONS

Faith of our fathers! Faber, 1849. St. Catherine. P348, E393.

God, the Lord, a King remaineth (Ps. 93). Keble, 1839. Bryn Calfaria. P90.

Hark! hark, my soul! Faber, 1854. Pilgrims. P426, E472.

O come and mourn with me awhile. Faber, 1849. St. Cross. P192, E74.

13. Nineteenth-Century British Hymnody: General

Technical histories of hymnody arrange the vast hymnic output of nineteenth-century Britain in such categories as (1) the Broad Church School, (2) the Evangelical School, and (3) the Anglican High Church School. To trace such currents is beyond the scope of this listing. However, it should be remarked that we owe a great debt of gratitude to Britain for the following hymns of proven worth.

IN THE TEN HYMNALS CITED

Abide with me. Lyte, 1847. Eventide. P64, E467.

Angels, from the realms of glory. Montgomery, 1816. Regent Square. P168, E28.

As with gladness men of old. William C. Dix, c. 1858. Dix. P174, E52.

Come, ye thankful people, come. Alford, 1844. St. George's, Windsor. P525, E137.

Eternal Father, strong to save. Whiting, 1860. Melita. P521, E512.

For all the saints. How, 1864. Sine Nomine. P425, E126.

For the beauty of the earth. Pierpoint, 1864. Dix. P2, E296.

Hail to the Lord's Anointed. Montgomery, 1821. Rockport. P146, E545.

Here, O my Lord, I see Thee face to face. Bonar, 1855. Morecambe, P442; Penitentia, E208.

I heard the voice of Jesus say. Bonar, 1846. Vox Dilecti. P280, E424.

Just as I am, without one plea. Elliott, 1836. WOODWORTH. P272, E409.

Nearer, my God, to Thee. Adams, 1840. BETHANY. P326, E465.

Now the day is over. Baring-Gould, 1865. MERRIAL. P51, E172.

O worship the King. Grant, 1833. LYONS, P26; HANOVER, E288.

Onward, Christian soldiers. Baring-Gould, 1864. ST. GERTRUDE. P350, E557.

Praise, my soul, the King of heaven. Lyte, 1834. LAUDA ANIMA (BENEDIC ANIMA MEA). P31, E282.

Saviour, again to Thy dear name. Ellerton, 1866. ELLERS. P77, E487.

Take my life, and let it be consecrated. Havergal, 1874. HENDON, P310; HOLLINGSIDE, E408.

The Church's one Foundation. Stone, 1866. AURELIA. P437, E396.

The King of love my Shepherd is. Baker, 1868. ST. COLUMBA. P106, E345.

There is a green hill far away. Alexander, 1848. MEDITATION. P202, E65.

We give Thee but Thine own. How, 1858. SCHUMANN, P312; YATTENDON 46, E481.

IN NINE OF THE HYMNALS

At even, when the sun was set. Twells, 1868. ANGELUS. P55, E168.

Come, ye disconsolate. Moore, 1816. CONSOLATION (WEBBE). P373, E483.

Crown Him with many crowns. Bridges, 1851. DIADEMATA. P213, E352.

Fight the good fight. Monsell, 1863. PENTECOST. P359, E560.

God the Omnipotent! King, who ordainest. Chorley, 1842. RUSSIAN HYMN. P487, E523.

I think when I read that sweet story. Jemima Luke, 1841. LUKE (SWEET STORY). P460, E246.

In the cross of Christ I glory. Bowring, 1825. RATHBUN. P195, E336.

Jesus calls us. Alexander, 1852. GALILEE. P269, E566.

Lord, speak to me. Havergal, 1872. CANONBURY, P298; WILDERNESS, E574.

O day of rest and gladness. Christopher Wordsworth, 1862. MENDEBRAS, P70; WOODBIRD, E474.

O Jesus, I have promised. Bode, 1868. ANGEL'S STORY, P307; LLANFYLLIN, E570.

O Jesus, Thou art standing. How, 1867. ST. HILDA (ST. EDITH). P266, E407.

O Love that wilt not let me go. Matheson, 1882. ST. MARGARET. P400, E458.

O Word of God Incarnate. How, 1867. MUNICH. P251, E402.

Once in royal David's city. Alexander, 1848. IRBY. P462, E236.

Our blest Redeemer ere He breathed. Auber, 1829. ST. CUTHBERT. E368.

Saviour, breathe an evening blessing. Edmeston, 1820. EVENING PRAYER (Stebbins), P54; VESPER HYMN, E178.

Saviour, teach me, day by day. Leeson, 1842. ORIENTIS PARTIBUS, P457; BUCKLAND, E428.

Ten thousand times ten thousand. Henry Alford, 1867. ALFORD. P427, E590.

The day Thou gavest, Lord, is ended. Ellerton, 1870. ST. CLEMENT. P59, E179.

Thou, whose almighty word. Marriott, c. 1813. MOSCOW (ITALIAN HYMN). E272.

ADDITIONAL SELECTIONS

The Head that once was crowned with thorns. Kelly, 1820. ST. MAGNUS. P211, E106.

14. Twentieth-Century British Hymnody

British hymns written during this century have in the main the same emphases as twentieth-century American hymnody. Outstanding hymns by recent British writers like Housman, Struther, Dearmer, and Briggs are rapidly reaching the pages of our newer hymnals.

IN NINE OF THE HYMNALS

In Christ there is no East or West. Oxenham, 1908. ST. PETER, P479; McKEE, E263.

ADDITIONAL SELECTIONS

Christ is the world's true Light. Briggs, 1931. St. Joan. P492, E258.

Father eternal, Ruler of creation. Housman, 1919. Langham. P486, E532.

I bind my heart this tide. Watt, 1907. Fealty. P286.

Lord of all hopefulness, Lord of all joy. Struther, 1933. Slane. E363.

O God of earth and altar. G. K. Chesterton, 1906. Llangloffan, P511; King's Lynn, E521.

O Son of Man, our Hero strong and tender. Fletcher, c. 1924. Charterhouse. P217, E364.

Turn back, O man, forswear thy foolish ways. Bax, 1916. Old 124th. P490, E536.

15. Nineteenth-Century American Hymnody

The first full century of this new nation's life witnessed the pioneer expansion to the West, the frightful civil struggle, and the growth of our industrial might. From the Church of this young country came the hymns which follow.

IN THE TEN HYMNALS CITED

Away in a manger. Anon., c. 1884. Mueller, P157; Cradle Song, E43.

It came upon the midnight clear. Sears, 1849. Carol. P160, E19.

My faith looks up to Thee. Palmer, 1830. Olivet. P378, E449.

O little town of Bethlehem. Brooks, 1868. St. Louis. P171, E21.

IN NINE OF THE HYMNALS

City of God, how broad and far. Johnson, 1860. Richmond. P436, E386.

Dear Lord and Father of mankind. Whittier, 1872. Rest. P416, E435.

I love Thy Kingdom, Lord. Dwight, 1800. St. Thomas. P435, E388.

O brother man, fold to thy heart thy brother. Whittier, 1848. Welwyn, P474; Intercessor, E493.

O Zion, haste, thy mission high. Thomson, 1868. TIDINGS. P491.

Once to every man and nation. Lowell, 1845. EBENEZER (TON-Y-BOTEL). P361, E519.

Stand up, stand up for Jesus. Duffield, 1858. WEBB. P349, E562.

ADDITIONAL SELECTIONS

Fling out the banner! Doane, 1848. WALTHAM. P506, E259.

Now on land and sea descending. Samuel Longfellow, 1859. VESPER HYMN. P67.

O beautiful for spacious skies. Bates, 1893. MATERNA. P510.

O Master, let me walk with Thee. Gladden, 1879. MARYTON. P304, E572.

"Thy Kingdom come," on bended knee. Hosmer, 1891. ST. FLAVIAN. P484, E391.

We are living, we are dwelling. Coxe, 1840. BLAENHAFREN. P356.

16. Nineteenth-Century Gospel Songs

Mainly through the influence of the Moody-Sankey revival campaigns, the last third of the century produced the gospel songs which achieved great popularity in some denominations and in certain sections of the country.

ADDITIONAL SELECTIONS

All the way my Saviour leads me. Crosby, 1875. ALL THE WAY. P365.

He leadeth me. Gilmore, 1862. HE LEADETH ME (AUGHTON). P338, E426.

I am Thine, O Lord. Crosby, 1875. I AM THINE. P320.

I need Thee every hour. Hawks, 1872. NEED. P324, E438.

I love to tell the story. Katherine Hankey, 1866. HANKEY. P383.

Tell me the old, old story. Hankey, 1866. EVANGEL. P403.

What a Friend we have in Jesus. Scriven, c. 1855. WHAT A FRIEND (ERIE). P385, E422.

17. Twentieth-Century American Hymnody

Interest in the Kingdom of God, the stirring of social conscience, concern for deeper worship, prayer for world friendship and peace

—these are some emphases found in contemporary American hymnody.

IN NINE OF THE HYMNALS

Rise up, O men of God! Merrill, 1911. FESTAL SONG. P352, E535.

Where cross the crowded ways of life. North, 1903. GERMANY (GARDINER). P507, E498.

ADDITIONAL SELECTIONS

All beautiful the march of days. Wile, 1912. FOREST GREEN. P96.

Eternal God, whose power upholds. Tweedy, 1929. FOREST GREEN, P485; WELLINGTON SQUARE, E265.

God of grace and God of glory. Fosdick, 1930. CWM RHONDDA, P358; MANNHEIM, E524.

God of our life, through all the circling years. Kerr, 1917. SANDON. P108.

Hope of the world, Thou Christ of great compassion. Harkness, 1953. DONNE SECOURS. P291.

Joyful, joyful, we adore Thee. Van Dyke, 1907. HYMN TO JOY, P21; ALLELUIA, E281.

O Holy City, seen of John. Bowie, 1909. MORNING SONG. P508, E494.

The light of God is falling. Benson, 1910. GREENLAND. P482.

They cast their nets in Galilee. Percy, 1924. GEORGETOWN. P421, E437.

This is my Father's world. Babcock, 1901. TERRA BEATA. P101.

CHAPTER 6 *Gospel Songs:*
Their Influence on
American Hymn Singing

For approximately one hundred years the churches of America have felt the influence of gospel songs on their congregational singing. The extent of this influence has varied from denomination to denomination. Those groups with an established liturgy and strong musical traditions like the Lutheran and Episcopal have not felt the impress as much as denominations like the Methodist, Baptist, and Presbyterian. In some of these latter denominations, gospel songs, in Dr. Louis Benson's words, "took possession of the Sunday schools, Christian Endeavor societies and devotional services, and encouraged a generation to grow up largely without the help and inspiration of great hymns. To many of these the tone of Church Praise seems still to lack the go and vivacity to which they had grown accustomed; and Gospel Hymns, old or new, keep knocking at the church gates for admission."[1]

The strong effect of gospel songs and singing has therefore produced a tension which has been felt and perhaps will always be felt by hymnal editorial committees and by everyone who desires to select hymns with conscientiousness. The following analogy may help to illustrate our predicament. Let us suppose that several dynamic American literary critics and lecturers had gone up and down the land around 1900 and so captivated the attention of public school literature teachers and officials that thereafter these instructors taught mainly the novels of men like Mark Twain, James Fenimore Cooper, and Booth Tarkington. A few teachers might slip in Milton's sonnet "On His Blindness" and some mention of Shakespeare's "Hamlet," but in the main the diet would be limited to the American novel. Several generations of American school children would have been deprived of their heritage in English and American literature.

Through the phenomenal evangelistic campaigns of Moody and Sankey, of Billy Sunday and Rodeheaver during the early years of this century, and more lately of Billy Graham and George Beverly Shea, gospel songs have come to the forefront—and remained there—in the hymnody of many local congregations. There are good and bad gospel songs just as there are superior and inferior American novels. My main point is to show that we now have in many denominations Sunday school superintendents, teachers, ministers, and musicians who, like our hypothetical literature students, have frequently not received their full heritage. Their hymnody is fragmentary through no fault of their own.

The heartening fact is that most major denominations in America have produced standard hymnals in the past thirty years which are fairly adequate anthologies of Christian hymnody. The concerned leadership of these groups can better communicate the contents of their hymnals to their people if they have a clear understanding of the place of gospel songs in American church life. Hence, let us ask: Where and how did gospel songs originate, just what is a gospel song (text and music), what value shall we place on them, and how shall we use them in our local churches?

First, where and how did gospel songs as a type originate?

The practice of singing the Good News of Christ is as old as Christianity itself. Within the lifetime of Paul the early Christians sang hymns concerning the gospel which probably included "Awake, O sleeper, and arise from the dead, and Christ shall give you light." (Ephesians 5:14, R.S.V.) Stephen the Sabaite tells in the eighth century of the compassion of Christ in a hymn from which Dr. Neale drew the idea of the text, "Art thou weary, art thou languid."

Thousands were led to Christian commitment during the 1700's by the marvelous singing of the Wesleyan revival. Watts' eighteenth-century hymn, "When I survey the wondrous cross," considered by many to be the greatest English hymn, contains the fullness of the gospel. Such facts indicate, first of all, that the expression of the Christian gospel in song is not the special prerogative of the class of songs known as "gospel songs." While there may be no one who would contend for this position, there are many who by implication and practice feel that gospel songs are almost the sole vehicle available for expressing the gospel call.

The gospel song as a type of hymnody is mainly an American phenomenon of the later nineteenth and early twentieth centuries. It had its roots in the Kentucky revivals during the first years of the eighteenth century and also in the early songbooks of the YMCA movement which began in the 1840's in England and the 1850's in America. About this same time a long series of Sunday school songbooks was written by men like Bradbury ("Sweet hour of prayer" and "He leadeth me"), Fischer ("I love to tell the story"), Lowry ("Shall we gather at the river"), and Bliss ("Let the lower lights be burning"). In 1865 William Booth began his tent meeting in Whitechapel in England, leading to the later formation of the Salvation Army which soon used gospel songs in abundance.

In 1870 Dwight L. Moody, then connected with the YMCA, met Ira D. Sankey at the Indianapolis YMCA convention and claimed him as his song leader. Moody, unable to tell one tune from another, decided to use the Lowry-Bliss type of music because he had observed its effect on the masses. After a spectacular evangelistic campaign in the British Isles in the early seventies, Moody and Sankey returned to America for additional extensive campaigning. Their songs, carefully copyrighted, were issued from 1876 to 1891 in six volumes entitled *Gospel Hymns and Sacred Songs*, hence the familiar title "gospel hymns." In the great Moody meetings in the Brooklyn Rink and the old Pennsylvania Railroad depot in Philadelphia these songs were circulated in immense quantities, and enthusiasm for them spread throughout the country.

Each evangelist who followed Moody felt that he, too, must have his own songbook. Since Moody's hymns were copyrighted, the evangelists had to find writers and composers to furnish other gospel songs. Before long, commercial houses undertook to publish gospel song books. This highly lucrative enterprise continues to the present day with the annual publication of hundreds of thousands of gospel song books, with the promotion of gospel song singing by the wide circulation of periodical instructional literature, and by the use of singing conventions and radio quartets.

We can better understand the nature of gospel songs if in our minds we reconstruct a typical Moody-Sankey evangelistic meeting of the type which first launched gospel songs on their amazing career. In the autumn of 1875 Moody was invited to hold a campaign in Philadelphia. The enormous abandoned Pennsylvania Railroad freight depot (later used by John Wanamaker as his store) was the meeting place. A large platform, 13,000 chairs, huge banners with Bible verses, and other equipment were provided. Night after night for several months there came to this improvised auditorium tens of thousands of people. Desperate drunkards; cultured atheists; prominent citizens like Wanamaker and Stuart; churchmen old and young, musical and non-musical—people of all sorts and conditions poured in to hear the great preacher Moody and his magnetic song leader Sankey.

These meetings were not services of worship in the usual sense of the word. They were mass meetings, surcharged with emotion, designed to impress the lost souls with the message of the gospel. The focus was the unsaved. The urgent desire was decision for Christ now.

When we recall that these people lived at a time when public school music was in its very infancy, when there were only several symphony orchestras in the whole country, when broadcasting and recorded classical music were unknown, we can see more clearly why the songs had to be perfectly simple and easily caught. All kinds of denominational backgrounds were present in these mass meetings. The song leader was unable to count on any musical or cultural background whatsoever in the congregation. The music had to be immediately grasped, as many individuals might never return for a second impression.

We can almost see and hear Sankey sitting at his little portable reed organ singing, "There were ninety and nine," or "Softly and tenderly Jesus is calling," while the vast throng listened intently.

Later, after Moody's sermon, he might lead the large chorus choir on the platform in singing the verses and then, turning to the multitude, he would lead the simple chorus:

> Tell me the old, old story,
> Tell me the old, old story,
> Tell me the old, old story,
>   Of Jesus and His love.[2]

Such singing was undoubtedly impressive and spiritually powerful.

A precise definition of a gospel song is difficult to formulate because many of our so-called "standard" hymns manifest some of these same characteristics. Dr. Benson describes it as follows:

> The Gospel Hymn continues the form and manner of the old spiritual and is equally charged with emotion. It has a contagious melody, pathetic or ringing, a frequent march or dance rhythm, and that peculiar thinness of effect which comes of continuing the harmony unchanged through the bar. It makes use of solo effects, of repeats, of burdens and climacteric catchwords, with of course a generous use of "that most sociable of musical devices," the chorus. It is, in other words, the conventional type of music appealing to the crowd as distinguished from more thoughtful and cultivated people.[3]

Millions of people during the past century have had opportunity to test and accept or discard gospel songs. Most of our major hymnals which have made any serious attempt to be discriminatingly inclusive, rather than exclusive, have included some gospel songs. Listed below as samples are gospel songs which appear in each of three standard hymnals of denominations which serve the entire United States and Canada (*The Methodist Hymnal* 1932, *The Hymnary* of the United Church of Canada 1930, and *The Hymnbook* 1955, produced jointly by five Presbyterian or Reformed bodies):

> He leadeth me.
> I am Thine, O Lord.
> More love to Thee.
> I need Thee every hour.
> What a Friend we have in Jesus.

Jesus, keep me near the cross.
I love to tell the story.
Saviour! Thy dying love.

What are some of the objections which have been leveled at gospel songs from the standpoint of text? Here are two.

1. Certain gospel song texts are oversimplified. As was pointed out earlier, many of our gospel songs were first issued in one of scores of Sunday school songbooks which flooded the country in the latter part of the last century. For example, several million copies of Lowry's *Royal Diadem, Bright Jewels,* and *Pure Gold* were published for use in local Sunday schools and Sunday school conventions. While these gospel songs have since appealed to millions of adult minds, they frequently were first issued for the child mind.

"Tell me the old, old story" was written, according to its author, Miss Hankey, when she was "weak and weary" after an illness. She realized that simple thoughts in simple words are all that most people can bear in sickness.

Such considerations for the mental limitation of children, the ill, and the unlettered led many authors to strive to be plain and obvious in their gospel song texts.

Simplicity, clarity, and directness, of course, are virtues in hymns as well as in sermons. Laymen with several university degrees appreciate this as much as a humble laborer with only a high school diploma or less. However, keeping in mind the average intelligence and culture of American congregations, we run a serious risk of not challenging, even of boring, many earnest Christians by using hymn texts which, though sacred, lack the kind of logical development and spiritual challenge found, for example, in many sermons.

To be specific, I have scrutinized the faces of scores of congregations engaged in singing this gospel song:

I can hear my Saviour calling,
I can hear my Saviour calling,
I can hear my Saviour calling,
    "Take thy cross and follow, follow Me."

Where He leads me I will follow,
Where He leads me I will follow,
Where He leads me I will follow,
   I'll go with Him, with Him all the way.[4]

All too frequently during the singing of this song I have observed wandering, vacant stares on the faces of the congregation. Why? Although the people were willing Christians, the text, while factual, simply did not hold their interest. The author had a good idea but he did not develop it. Repetition up to a point is a legitimate device for learning truth. After that point it ceases to have value.

By contrast, I have rarely seen a congregation thoughtlessly sing the following hymn, which deals likewise with the thought of following Christ:

Lead on, O King Eternal:
  We follow, not with fears;
For gladness breaks like morning
  Where'er Thy face appears;
Thy cross is lifted o'er us;
  We journey in its light:
The crown awaits the conquest;
  Lead on, O God of might.[5]

This very popular and easily sung hymn will give to any attentive singer a thought-provoking concept of Christian discipleship.

Christian leaders have a responsibility to build up their followers into mature disciples of Christ who have a clear, defensible reason for their faith. Well-developed texts of hymns are educational tools which should be used with discrimination.

2. Some gospel songs give an erroneous impression of Christian truth. I have in mind two familiar gospel songs. I hesitate to criticize them because I know that they have been hallowed by long use, and yet I feel that they should be re-evaluated. The first song text is as follows:

Pass me not, O gentle Saviour,
  Hear my humble cry;

> While on others Thou art smiling,
>   Do not pass me by.
> Saviour, Saviour,
>   Hear my humble cry;
> While on others Thou art calling,
>   Do not pass me by.[6]

Jesus said, "Him that cometh to me I will in no wise cast out."[7] While some religious thinkers may be able to justify this song by Fanny Crosby, it is entirely possible that many singers could gain the impression that our Master was reluctant and capricious and that He might overlook some genuine penitent in need of His mercy and salvation.

A much truer picture of our Master's love and concern is found in this hymn text:

> O Jesus, Thou art standing
> Outside the fast-closed door,
> In lowly patience waiting
> To pass the threshold o'er . . .[8]

The second gospel song for discussion is "Holy Spirit, faithful Guide," written in 1858 by the New York State farmer, Marcus Wells. Here is the last stanza of this rather widely used song:

> When our days of toil shall cease,
> Waiting still for sweet release,
> Nothing left but heaven and prayer,
> Wondering if our names are there,
> Wading deep the dismal flood,
> Pleading naught but Jesus' blood,—
> Whisper softly, "Wanderer, come!
> Follow me, I'll guide thee home."

The phrase, "wondering if our names are there," does not sound like Paul in Romans 8:38-39: "For I am sure that neither death, nor life . . . will be able to separate us from the love of God in Christ Jesus our Lord."[9] A much more Christian prospect for old age is given in a stanza of "How firm a foundation" used in some hymnals:

> E'en down to old age all My people shall prove
> My sovereign, eternal, unchangeable love;
> And when hoary hairs shall their temples adorn,
> Like lambs they shall still in My bosom be borne.[10]

Frequently it is the tune of a gospel song rather than the text which attracts the affection of singers. And this is precisely what a hymn tune should not do. Its purpose should be to underscore the intent of the text so that there is deeper understanding of the thought. In the better gospel songs, the music does reinforce the drive of the ideas but in the inferior examples the effect of the tune is negative and positively detrimental.

A British musician, Dr. Harvey Grace, in his *The Complete Organist*, gives an imaginary conversation between an organist and his rector about this matter of gospel song music. The rector asks who is to decide that these tunes are bad. The organist replies,

> Most educated people are quite clear as to the difference between the good and bad in literary and pictorial art. In music, the distinction is equally clear to all who have received a musical training worth the name. They, surely, should be arbiters enough for you. Do you realise, too, that music has its grammar—a code of rules as definite in most cases as those governing language? You would be horrified if I suggested that the choir should sing a hymn, the first lines of which ran:
> > "I is a awful sinner,
> > And you be just the same."
> You would point out that although the lines contain a statement about which there can be no dispute, the diction is so crude, and the grammar so hopeless as to render the hymn unfit for use, and I should agree with you. Do you know that most hymn tunes of the popular type contain breaches of musical grammar quite as excruciating to a musician as the above lines are to you?[11]

How shall we evaluate gospel songs as a group? In the first place, we should realize that opinions concerning the relative merits and proper use of gospel songs vary extremely. Dr. Waldo Selden Pratt said more than fifty years ago in his *Musical Ministries*:

Much of the criticism of these "Hymns" is reckless, both because it fails to note the fact that different grades of artistic beauty in poetry and music have always been required among Christians of differing degrees of culture, and also because it assails indiscriminately a class of hymns and tunes that is not homogeneous enough to be either approved or condemned in bulk.

But, on the other hand, the common defense of even the best of the "Gospel Hymns" is often weak, especially when it appeals chiefly to their quick outward success among masses of people who are plainly thoughtless and shallow. Both the attack and the defense should be more careful.

The assailants of the system have sometimes weakened their case by basing it too exclusively on reasons of taste, without showing how vulgarity is dangerous because more or less false, and by failing to leave room for practices that are provisional and transitional and that are therefore defensible in their place.

The defenders of this popular hymnody have a right to urge that hymnody must adapt itself to actual conditions, that the immature and uncultivated cannot be driven by force into a full appreciation of the most highly poetic hymns or the most highly musical tunes; but they often very gravely underestimate the capacity of the popular mind to rise above vulgar embodiments of truth and to shake itself free from perverted sentimentality, and they constantly mistake the zest of animal enjoyment in a rub-a-dub rhythm or the shout of childish pleasure in a "catchy" refrain for real religious enthusiasm.[12]

In the second place, we should realize that present-day leaders in local churches face problems in the choice of congregational music different from the song leaders in evangelistic enterprises. Most people attending the usual church gatherings have been members for years, having embraced the Christian way long ago. Many of the youth sing or play in the excellent public school choir or orchestra. It is not inferred that we should never sing gospel songs. I am suggesting that we could well be more discerning in the kind of gospel songs we sing and the type of occasion when we announce them. It is conceivable that a song written specifically with adult lost profligates in mind might not be entirely appropriate for a child in the Junior Department who since infancy has been nurtured in a Christian home and Sunday school.

Third, the proportion of gospel songs in the repertoire of congregations will vary from church to church. It will depend partly on the tastes and inclinations of the minister and organist. The educational process must take into consideration the affection which the man in the pew has for gospel songs.

Also it is hoped that evangelists and their musicians will follow the lead of men like the Wesleys who had a serious educational approach to their use of music. If present-day converts were given solid fiber in their evangelistic texts and music, they could be sent to established churches and there hear the same fine music.

In conclusion, we must recognize that gospel hymns are a part of the heritage of American church music. The better ones have a distinct place in assisting the evangelistic enterprises of the Church. However, we must keep a perspective of the total output of Christian hymns and see that our congregations receive a balanced selection of all worthy hymns. Most congregational singing is designed to express the worship of people who have already begun the Christian pilgrimage, whose chief end is to glorify God and to enjoy Him forever.

Part Three

THE HYMNAL

CHAPTER 7 *The Structure and Use of Hymnals*

A hymnal is an anthology of hymns, to be used privately or publicly for devotional purposes by Christians. At least three trends may be traced in the hymnals of this generation. First, there has been a healthy move toward a core of hymnody, common to the major denominations. The ecumenical spirit abroad in Christendom has been a major factor in this development. The list of basic hymns in chapter 5 is graphic illustration of this fact. Second, most hymnals contain a more balanced representation of the main streams of church song, drawn from the major periods of church history. Third, where there is a distinctive denominational heritage in hymnody, this has been affirmed by generous inclusion of this type of music. For instance, the Presbyterian *Hymnbook* of 1955 includes about eighty metrical psalms.

Thousands of different hymnals have been edited and their variety is endless. Some of them have had enormous circulation like the British hymnal *Hymns Ancient and Modern,* first issued in the nineteenth century, with an estimated circulation of over sixty million copies. By contrast, Dr. Louis Benson's collection of his own *Hymns* was privately printed with three hundred copies. *The Church Hymnary* of the Presbyterian churches of the British Commonwealth has seven hundred and seven hymns while the newly revised A *Hymnal for Friends* has only one hundred and seventy-six. Most hymnals are of ordinary book size. However, the French Evangelical Protestant hymnal *Louange et Prière* is quite manageable in one's side coat pocket and it includes not only texts but complete music. Even smaller is the little vest-pocket

Wayside Hymnal with words and music published by the Forward Movement of the Episcopal Church.

Most standard hymnals in America are denominational collections, edited and published officially by denominational boards specifically for use by congregations in these particular denominations. Some of these church agencies also publish a series of hymnals graded to suit age groups of children and youth. *Christian Worship* is an instance of a hymnal issued jointly by two major denominations—Disciples of Christ and the Northern Baptist Convention. In Japan and China, hymnals have been prepared to serve a number of national denominational groups. For use in multi-lingual gatherings, the polyglot *Cantate Domino* hymnal was prepared by the World's Student Christian Federation. Each hymn is translated into three languages, with a total of twenty-three tongues included in the hymnal. It is used in the assemblies of the World Council of Churches and in most international Christian gatherings.

Numerous specialized hymnals have been created. *Hymns of the Rural Spirit* is a collection of one hundred and twenty-three hymns designed to express the religious interests of farming communities. Under the auspices of the National Council of the Churches of Christ in America the *Fellowship Hymnal* was prepared for use in mental hospitals, correctional and penal institutions, Veterans Administration hospitals, and juvenile correctional institutions. The British Broadcasting Company, finding the hymns on its daily and Sunday broadcasts very popular, published *The BBC Hymnbook* mainly for use in the homes of Britain. For those who love Easter, Summer, Harvest, and Christmas carols, *The Oxford Book of Carols* is a uniquely fine collection.

Some hymnals have interesting unique features. *The Book of Praise* of the Presbyterian Church in Canada and *Christian Hymns*, sponsored by the Christian Foundation of Columbus, Indiana, have at the head of each hymn a Scripture verse which succinctly summarizes the thought of the hymn. For organists and pianists *The Brethren Hymnal* of the Church of the Brethren provides a system of symbols in the musical score of each hymn to indicate the sections of the tune which may be omitted when shortened introductions to the hymn are desired. *The Book of Praise* of the Presbyterian Church in Canada and *The Christian Science Hymnal* both give exact metronome markings to indicate the precise speed at which the hymn should be played. In *The Scottish Psalter 1929*, the music of the psalm is at the top of the page and the text is at the bottom. Each page of the Psalter is cut across the middle, like the old-fashioned barn door, so that it is possible, for example, to have the hundred and fourth tune open at the top of the page with the text for the Seventy-second Psalm open at the bottom of the page. Several hymnals (The Episcopal *Hymnal 1940* and the Presbyterian *Hymnbook*) have provided spirally bound books for pianists and organists.

Hymnal Patterns

Most hymnals are arranged according to one of the following two patterns:

1. *Topical grouping.* Hymnals like *The Hymnbook* (Presbyterian 1955) and *The Methodist Hymnal* have the entire body of hymns sorted and located according to a framework of doctrine, function, or occasion. A glance at the following outline of the contents of *The Hymnbook* (Presbyterian) shows the completeness of the coverage of the faith and work of the Presbyterian Church.

WORSHIP

Adoration and Praise
Morning
Evening
The Lord's Day
Closing

GOD

God the Father
  His Eternity and Power
  In Nature
  His Love and Fatherhood
  His Presence

Jesus Christ
  Adoration and Praise

His Advent
His Birth
His Epiphany
His Life and Ministry
His Triumphal Entry
His Passion and Atonement
His Resurrection
His Ascension
His Presence
His Coming in Glory

The Holy Spirit

The Holy Trinity

THE HOLY SCRIPTURES

LIFE IN CHRIST

The Call of Christ
Repentance and Forgiveness
Discipleship and Service
Dedication and Consecration
Stewardship
Hope and Aspiration
Pilgrimage and Guidance
Loyalty and Courage
Trial and Conflict
Faith and Assurance
Prayer and Intercession
Love
Joy
Peace
The Life Everlasting

THE CHURCH

The Church
The Lord's Supper

Holy Baptism
Marriage
The Christian Home
Hymns for the Young
Hymns for Youth
Christian Fellowship

THE KINGDOM OF GOD ON EARTH

Brotherhood
World Friendship and Peace
Missions
The City
The Nation

MISCELLANEOUS

The Dedication of a Church
The Ministry
Travelers
Thanksgiving
The New Year

Kenneth L. Parry in his little book *Christian Hymns* (SCM Press) arranges his chapters along a similar topical outline and discusses certain hymns which ordinarily fall in these sections, dealing with them chronologically.

2. *The Church year.* Denominations using a more liturgical form of worship frequently arrange a considerable section of the book according to the Christian year. The Episcopal *Hymnal 1940*, for example, begins with Advent hymns and continues through Christmas, Epiphany, and right through the Trinity season. Then the second section of the book, containing general hymns, is organized by topical grouping. Incidentally, at the end of each topical section in this and other hymnals is a list of additional hymns in the hymnal bearing on this particular topic.

Page Format

Hymnals are generally published with full music score, and American hymnals ordinarily have most or all of the text between the musical staves.[1]

As one looks at a page in a hymnal, the name of the author of the words is on the upper left-hand side. The date following his name is the year in which the text was written. Occasionally, when this cannot be surely established, the first publication date is mentioned. If the author is unknown, then the hymnal in which the text originated is given. Similar information about the composer, date, and book source of the tune is found at the upper right-hand side of the page.

Next, at the top of the page, we find two items of information about the music: first, the tune name, and, second, the meter of the tune. Each of these is discussed later in this chapter.

Somewhere on the page will be found the name of the topical grouping as outlined earlier in the sample table of contents, such as "Evening Hymns" or "The Nativity of Christ." This enables a leader in search of a hymn dealing with a given theme to thumb through a section of related material and to know the major emphasis of this group of hymns.

Certain other instructions are sometimes given. When the editors do not have room for printing an alternate tune on the opposite page and yet feel that one should be suggested, this advice is usually added as a footnote under the hymn.

Occasionally editors will give interpretive indications at the beginning of the hymns. For example, *The Hymnal* (Presbyterian 1933) and the Episcopal *Hymnal 1940* both include such phrases as "Without dragging," "In moderate time," "With dignity," and "In unison." These remarks help both organist and congregation to approach the hymn with a specific attitude of interpretation.

Service Music

In addition to the main body of hymns, most hymnals have a section at the end of the book devoted to congregational chants and to choral aids to worship.

1. *Chants.* Many hymnbooks (such as *The Hymnbook*, Presbyterian 1955, the Episcopal *Hymnal 1940*, and *The Methodist Hymnal*) include Anglican chant settings of the usual morning and evening canticles such as Benedictus es, Domine; Jubilate;

Te Deum; Nunc Dimittis; and Magnificat. Of course their use is mandatory in the Episcopal services, and there is a complete and varied collection of Anglican musical settings in the Episcopal *Hymnal 1940*. While their use is not widespread in the Presbyterian church, they are a valuable addition. A clear, brief explanation of the principles of chanting may be found on pages 697-698 of the Episcopal *Hymnal 1940*. A more extensive set of directions for chanting is contained in *The Oxford American Psalter* (Oxford) by Ray Brown. An accepted method of chanting is illustrated by an authoritative recording, *Music of the Liturgy in English* (Columbia ML 4528).

2. *Choral aids to worship*. The efforts of liturgically minded leaders in the so-called non-liturgical churches to enrich the worship led to the provision of many brief items of music such as Calls to Worship, Introits, Scripture and Prayer Responses, Offertory Sentences, and Amens. Many of these can be sung by the congregation as well as by the choir.

3. *Other aids to worship*. In denominations such as the Lutheran, Methodist, and Presbyterian, the hymnal also includes liturgical material such as outlines of orders of worship, Old and New Testament passages, opening sentences and prayers, creeds and the like. These are omitted from the Episcopal *Hymnal 1940* since *The Book of Common Prayer* is provided in the pew racks alongside the hymnal.

Indexes

A variety of indexes is provided in most standard hymnals to permit efficient use of the contents. Here are the usual ones:

1. A *table of contents* (a sample one was given earlier in the chapter).

2. *Index of first lines*. In most standard hymnals, the hymns are designated by their first lines rather than by a separate title; hence the main index for locating hymns is called Index of First Lines.

3. *Index of tunes*. Every tune worth its salt has a name. There are many explanations for tune names. For example, a tune may be named after the first words of the hymn with which it was

originally associated (LOBE DEN HERREN meaning in German "Praise to the Lord"), the number of the psalm originally sung to it (OLD 100TH, OLD 124TH), the name of a place (ABERYSTWYTH, ST. PETERSBURG), the name of a saint (ST. COLUMBA, ST. PETER), or the name of a person (BEECHER, DARWALL's 148TH).[2]

4. *Metrical index.* For the uninitiated, this is the most complicated index. Its purpose is to facilitate judicious exchange of tunes and texts of similar meter. In this index all tunes which fit a particular metrical pattern are grouped together. By the tune name above each hymn is found a symbol like 7.6.7.6.D. or L.M. These numbers and abbreviations indicate the metrical framework of the text; in other words, these numbers tell the exact number of syllables per line or phrase. Since the tune of a particular text matches it, it usually means that it is possible—and sometimes desirable—to exchange a text and tune which have the same metrical pattern.

To illustrate, let us recall the familiar Doxology, "Praise God from whom all blessings flow." This is called the Long Meter Doxology because each of the four phrases has eight syllables. You might count these phrases in your memory right now. There are a number of Long Meter (L.M. or 8.8.8.8.) texts in the hymnal which could easily be sung to the Doxology tune, OLD HUNDREDTH. Try these: "Jesus shall reign where'er the sun" and "Sun of my soul, Thou Saviour dear." Now you might try the Doxology text to the tune DUKE STREET ("Jesus shall reign") or GERMANY ("Where cross the crowded ways of life"). Each of these combinations will work. However, not all of these are desirable, for reasons to be mentioned later.

The major use made of this metrical device is to substitute a familiar tune for an unfamiliar one when the leader of worship wants to use a particular text. He knows that his people can read and understand any English in the book, but he knows also that they may balk quite understandably at a tune they have never sampled before. Suppose, for example, the minister would like in a service of national thankgiving to use Dr. Merrill's stirring hymn beginning:

Not alone for mighty empire
Stretching far o'er land and sea,
Not alone for bounteous harvests,
Lift we up our hearts to Thee.[3]

In many hymnals this text is wedded either to the Welsh tune
HYFRYDOL, a very singable Welsh tune, or GENEVA, a modern
American melody. Suppose the congregation did not know either
of these tunes. The minister could retain the text and find another tune known to his people. He would see at a glance that
the pattern is 8.7.8.7.D. (D. means doubled, or 8.7.8.7.8.7.8.7.).
Looking at the Metrical Index of Tunes, in most hymnals he
would find the names of a dozen or more tunes of this type. He
would probably discard from consideration such 8.7.8.7.D. tunes
as "What a friend we have in Jesus" and "All the way my Saviour
leads me." The tune, HYMN TO JOY ("Joyful, joyful, we adore
Thee") and AUSTRIAN HYMN ("Glorious things of Thee are
spoken"), if known by the congregation, might suit the text acceptably. Many editors suggest in a note below this hymn that
AUSTRIAN HYMN is a good alternate tune.

A glance at any Metrical Index will reveal this simple arrangement. First, Short Meter (S.M. or 6.6.8.6.) and Short Meter
Doubled (S.M.D.) are listed. Then Common Meter (C.M. or
8.6.8.6.) and Common Meter Doubled are followed by Long
Meter and Long Meter Doubled. Then in rising serial order—for
example, from 3.8.6.5.6.3. up to 14.14.4.7.8.—tunes in various
metrical categories are found.

Several bits of advice could be offered regarding use of this
method of tune interchange:

(1) If possible, use the tune given with the text. Follow some
of the procedures outlined elsewhere in this book for introducing
unfamiliar tunes. It is stagnating to revert back to the few old
and tried favorites.

(2) When seeking a new tune, find a musical setting which
matches the mood and spirit of the text. One would never think
of matching the text, "O God, our Help in ages past" with the
tune SERENITY ("Immortal Love, forever full") or the text, "Once

to every man and nation" with the tune BRADBURY, "Saviour, like a Shepherd lead us."

It is interesting to note that the editor of *The Church Hymnary* did select TON-Y-BOTEL as the first musical setting for the hymn "What a Friend we have in Jesus"! It gives a rugged strength to this text.

(3) The accentual pattern of the text and tune must match. For example, the text "Gentle Mary laid her Child" and the tune AURELIA ("The Church's one Foundation") are both 7.6.7.6.D., but, speaking technically, one is trochaic and the other iambic. In other words, the text has the accent on syllables 1-3-5-7 and the tune throws the accent on syllables 2-4-6.

5. *Indexes of composers and authors and other sources.* In these two indexes all hymns are listed according to the names of the authors, translators, and sources of words, and according to composers, arrangers, and sources of tunes. When known, the birth and death dates are given and, sometimes, the nationality.

6. *Topical index.* This index lists the hymns under many subject headings. It is a valuable tool for a worship leader needing a hymn to develop a particular theme. It will be recalled that earlier in this chapter it was stated that hymns are grouped in most hymnals according to subject matter. For example, all hymns dealing mainly with the Sabbath (such as "O day of rest and gladness") are found together.

However, since many hymns have a number of subordinate but important emphases, this index helps locate them. Let us illustrate. In many hymnals "Joyful, joyful, we adore Thee" is located in a section entitled Worship: Adoration and Praise. Nevertheless, it has a strong nature emphasis. Therefore in many topical indexes it is probably found also under the section of Nature Hymns.

7. *Other indexes.* Other hymnals have specialized indexes such as the following: Scriptural Allusions, Foreign Titles of Hymns, Chronological Index, and Index of First Lines of *All* Stanzas.

A practical bit of advice should be offered. Supply enough hymnals in the pews so that every church member can have a copy to himself.

One final suggestion about hymnals. Every student of hymnology should have at least one hymnal of indubitable superiority even though it may not be his particular denomination's production. He will find refreshment in reading the superb texts and sitting at his piano playing the wonderful melodies. Let me suggest one or more of the following books—generally considered in the top bracket:

The English Hymnal with Tunes. (Oxford, 1906.)

Songs of Praise with Music. Enlarged Edition. (Oxford, 1931.)

The Church Hymnary. Revised Edition. Presbyterian. (Oxford, 1927.)

Congregational Praise. Congregational Union of England and Wales. (Independent Press, 1951.)

Service Book and Hymnal. Lutheran. (Augsburg Publishing House, 1958.)

Pilgrim Hymnal. (Pilgrim Press, 1958.)

Hymnal for Colleges and Schools. (Yale University Press, 1956.)

Part Four

THE LEADER OF WORSHIP

CHAPTER 8 *The Responsibility of the Leader of Worship for Hymn Singing*

Although the ideas of this chapter are addressed to the minister, since he leads the entire congregation in corporate worship, many suggestions also pertain to lay people who lead smaller groups in worship such as youth assemblies, church school departments, and women's groups.

A vital leadership in hymn singing can come only from one who loves hymns, who knows the spiritual values of congregational singing, and who uses hymns to strengthen his personal devotional life. Such affection for hymn singing cannot long remain hidden from his people. Here are some specific ways in which a minister can exercise his leadership in this sphere of worship: (1) his use of his personal hymnal, (2) his use of handbooks about hymns, (3) his choice of hymns, (4) his choice of proper stanzas, (5) the manner of announcing hymns, (6) his example during hymn singing, (7) his occasional quotation of hymns, (8) occasional talks or sermons based on hymns, (9) his use of hymn-anthems sung by choir or soloist, and (10) his use of certain hymns as counseling tools.

1. *The Leader's Use of a Personal Copy of the Hymnal*

In order to plan most helpfully for worship, many leaders purchase a personal copy of the hymnal. On the margin alongside each hymn they note the dates when it was used in their services. If the hymn is new, the date reminds them to repeat it in the near future. Such notations also prevent too frequent duplication of old favorites, furnish data for an annual study of the congregation's repertoire of hymns, and supply the incentive for further exploration of unfamiliar hymns.

Some ministers also mark each hymn with a key symbol which indicates the congregation's familiarity with or response to the hymn. The late Dr. Harry Myers of Central Theological Seminary in Japan gave me his personal copy of the *Japanese Hymnal*. Alongside almost every hymn is a check mark, circle, or cross indicating Dr. Myers' judgment of the worth and familiarity of that particular hymn. An organist or choir director would be glad to help the minister in evaluating the usability of each hymn.

Leaders should understand the structure of standard hymnals. (See chapter 7.) The table of contents gives the pattern. It will be discovered that hymns bearing on similar topics are grouped together in the body of the book. Thus, if a hymn of consecration is needed, a glance at the table of contents will show immediately where these particular hymns are to be found. Furthermore, all leaders should study the other indexes. The topical index, for example, is especially valuable because these pages give a cross-listing of hymns according to topics. By means of the metrical index it is possible in certain cases to substitute an unfamiliar tune for a melody known by the congregation. This is described in detail in chapter 7.

2. *The Leader's Use of Hymnal Handbooks*

The most effective leaders in hymn singing have stimulated their interest in the subject by the purchase of several good books on hymnology. Knowledge begets enthusiasm. Few approaches can equal hymn stories in interesting a congregation in hymn singing. I would start off with *The Story of Our Hymns*, by Haeussler. This volume is the handbook to *The Hymnal* of the Evangelical and Reformed Church. While many handbooks are available, this volume is one of the best. In it are the stories behind 481 hymns and tunes, most of which are widely known and loved in all Christian denominations. Biographical material regarding authors and composers is included. The information is well written and accurate. In addition to the hymn stories, there is also a practical essay on hymn playing.[1]

There is a minister who for years has followed the custom of reading during the week the stories of the three hymns chosen for the following Sunday morning service. He does not tell all of them to the congregation each Sunday but he has built up a wealth of personal knowledge and his congregation has caught a great deal of his enthusiasm for hymns. Dr. Gillman in *The Evolution of the English Hymn* expresses the value of these hymn stories in these words:

> A hymn book is a transcript from real life . . . the heart of the Christian Church is revealed in its hymns; and if we will take the trouble to relate them to the circumstances that gave them birth, we shall find that they light up with a new meaning and have fresh power to help us in our daily lives.[2]

In addition to acquiring knowledge of individual hymns, the leader would profit by reading a continuous narrative on the use of hymns. For the fascinating history of congregational singing through the Christian era, one could start with *The Story of the Church's Song*, by Millar Patrick. This book is one of the best historical narratives and originally was based on *The Church Hymnary*, which is perhaps the greatest Presbyterian hymnal in the world.[3] *The Hymnody of the Christian Church* by Dr. Louis Benson is a collection of six magnificent lectures delivered originally to theological students. It is a classic in the subject.[4]

3. *The Choice of Hymns*

The selection of hymns is the minister's responsibility except in unusual circumstances. It may be frequently advisable for him to consult his musician regarding the appropriateness of the tune. Certainly he should send the list of hymns to the organist in ample time to permit adequate practice. Further, it is not kind to shift to another hymn at the last minute in the service since it embarrasses many amateur organists to be asked to read at sight an unexpected hymn.

Here are some guiding principles for selection:

(1) Select hymns with worthy texts and tunes. Many sanctuaries and church school departments have fine hymnals. Others,

unfortunately, have not yet been able to purchase good ones. If you have a first-rate hymnal, the problem of worthy texts has largely been solved by the hymnal editors. They have eliminated the worthless hymns. Leaders who use other hymnals should exercise care in the choice of texts. The qualities of good texts and tunes are described in chapter 4.

Public school music education is based on the use of music of superior quality. The church should do no less.

(2) For genuine worship experiences, select familiar hymns. The members of your group cannot easily think of the ideas of the hymn when they are following the devious routes of a strange tune. The average person cannot readily praise God when he or she is distracted by the mechanics of note-reading, any more than a novice can enjoy the landscape when driving a car for the first time.

Therefore, your people can worship most naturally through familiar hymns. When you must use an unfamiliar but appropriate hymn in a regular service, rehearse a special group of singers beforehand, if possible, so that they can help in leading it. Announce the hymn so that group participation is encouraged, and have the tune played clearly. Even better, set aside an occasional informal period when the new tunes can be taught.

(3) Select hymns bearing on the worship topic. If the topic of the service and sermon is "faith," you would obviously use such hymns as "My faith looks up to Thee," "How firm a foundation," "Faith of our fathers," or similar hymns. The Topical Index will help in this intelligent selection.

(4) Select hymns which are emotionally appropriate. Most of our worship follows a pattern of emotional experiences. Hymns can help express these emotions. A hymn of adoration, like "Holy, Holy, Holy! Lord God Almighty," usually opens this service. The sermon is usually preceded by a hymn bearing on its thought. After the sermon it is usually appropriate to sing a hymn of dedication. Do not carelessly use hymns which call for a tremendous commitment unless you feel that your group is emotionally prepared to mean what it sings. I have in mind such hymns as "Faith of our

fathers, we will be true to thee till death," and "Jesus, I my cross have taken."

(5) Select hymns adapted to the average age of your group. Some hymns, like "Fairest Lord Jesus" and "For the beauty of the earth," can be sung together by Christians of all age levels. Hymns like "Depth of mercy! can there be mercy still reserved for me?" and "Come, ye disconsolate" are more suited to the adult mind. Other hymns like "Now in the days of youth" express admirably the aspiration of young people. In so far as you can, select hymns which ring true to the experience and thought of your group.

(6) Select hymns which include the entire Christian experience. Do not be narrow or one-sided in your choice of hymns. Too often we sing about the starting point and the close of the Christian life and too rarely do we sing about the glorious pilgrimage between these points. Christian experience includes struggle with evil, adoration, courageous conduct, missions, redemption, hope. Our hymns should include these and all other aspects of the Christian life.

Hymnal editors winnow a half-million hymns to produce a hymnbook. The individual leader of worship by his intelligent choice of a single hymn completes this process, thus bringing the accumulated experience of Christendom to a focus in the act of musical worship.

4. Choosing Hymn Stanzas

Superior hymns are composed of a number of stanzas, each of which develops a particular idea. These stanzas are usually connected logically with each other and they rise to a climax of thought and feeling in the last stanza. Consequently it is usually wise to sing the entire hymn, if possible.

Hymns like "Come, Thou Almighty King" and "Ancient of Days," which devote a stanza to each Person of the Trinity, obviously lose their meaning if shortened. Of course people would miss a stanza of "The Lord's my Shepherd."

Actually many of our familiar hymns are abridged versions of much longer hymns or poems, some of which included scores of stanzas in the original form. "Dear Lord and Father of mankind," for example, is from a long poem of seventeen stanzas entitled "The Brewing of Soma." Many hymnals of former generations included hymns with dozens of stanzas. Nowadays editorial committees have reduced the great majority of hymns to an average length of three to five stanzas. These editors have carefully studied the originals and have kept only the most worthwhile units of thought.

There are many times, however, when it is feasible to omit certain stanzas. If this is necessary, be sure to omit only those stanzas which do not violate the sense. The difficulty frequently is that the selection of the omittable stanzas has to be made on the spur of the moment when a sermon or service has lasted longer than expected. An interesting aid in such situations is offered in *The Hymnal 1940* (Episcopal). Asterisks are added beside any stanza which may be omitted without destroying the over-all sense of the hymn. It is to be hoped that this practical aid will be copied by other hymnal committees.

We have all witnessed the careless omission of stanzas, such as singing the first and last stanzas of "In the cross of Christ." In most hymnals they are identical! I have also heard it reported that a minister announced the first stanza only of "A mighty Fortress is our God," which left the Devil in complete charge!

> For still our ancient foe
> Doth seek to work us woe;
> His craft and power are great;
> And, armed with cruel hate,
> On earth is not his equal.

The Episcopal hymnal, incidentally, by its asterisk system, suggests the possible omission of the last two stanzas of this great hymn, if necessary.

Worshipers on many occasions would welcome a judicious pruning of such long hymns as "O Zion, haste, thy mission" and "We've a story to tell to the nations," which are long hymns with many stanzas plus a chorus. One's spiritual pulse sometimes begins to wane as one enters the fourth or fifth stanza of such hymns. Other hymns like "How firm a foundation" and "For all the saints" frequently will have greater spiritual effectiveness after some careful abbreviation.

Instead of omitting stanzas of a long hymn, ministers have sometimes followed this procedure: if the hymn had, say, six stanzas, they have requested the congregation to sing the first three, to read aloud the fourth and fifth, and then to sing the final stanza. The writer has also seen this note in the bulletin of a large Brooklyn church under the announcement of a long hymn, "The choir alone will sing the third stanza."

Then, too, it is a good idea sometimes to have a congregation sing just one stanza of a hymn, and it need not always be the first or the last stanza. A service could be closed with the third stanza of "Abide with me," which begins with "I need Thy presence every passing hour." Upon occasion the second stanza only of "Dear Lord and Father of mankind" has been used. This one ends appropriately with "Let us, like them, without a word rise up and follow Thee." Or at Communion, just the third stanza of "Jesus, Thou Joy of loving hearts" could significantly express the worshiper's emotions with the words beginning "We taste Thee, O Thou living Bread."

Incidentally "stanza," not "verse," is the preferred term to use in speaking of a group of lines forming a unit of a hymn. A "verse," strictly speaking, is a single line of poetry.

5. *The Announcement of Hymns*

Many congregations have been trained to follow an order of service without any verbal announcement. The hymn numbers are included in the printed bulletin and are also listed on the hymn number board in front of the church. While this custom has its commendable features, it is certainly true that occasional verbal announcements of the hymns by the minister will definitely stimulate the singing.

Even though the hymns are listed in the bulletin, there are a number of preachers who, after making the announcements, occasionally introduce the sermon hymn with several well-chosen comments. Others sometimes do the same thing when announcing the final hymn.

Psychologically it is a big boost to congregational interest in singing to have a pleasant word of comment and encouragement just before singing. On a rainy Sunday evening, Dr. Theodore F. Adams, minister of the First Baptist Church of Richmond, introduced the opening hymn with some such statement as this: "The fact that this good-sized congregation turned out on a rainy night shows that you must love the Lord. We are all going to join now in singing 'Come, we that love the Lord, and let our joys be known.'" And they really sang! People who attend services in this particular church testify that the very method of announcing hymns makes them want to sing.

In announcing hymns, it is perhaps unwise to use a standard formula like "Let us sing to the praise of God hymn number 65." Many hymns are not addressed to God in praise. A number of them, like "Onward, Christian soldiers," are hymns of exhortation and admonition.

Also it should be urged that hymns be introduced by saying, "Let us sing," instead of by the question, "May we sing?"

If the hymns are regularly announced from the pulpit, it would probably be a good idea to vary the introductory comments, taking care to keep them dignified, concise, and challenging. A congregation once made a commendable effort to master a completely new hymn because the minister said something like this by way of introduction: "Although our final hymn is unfamiliar, I want to urge each of you to try to sing it because it expresses the thought of the sermon so completely."

A brief comment about the history of a hymn may focus the attention of the people upon the thought of the words. For example, in announcing "O for a thousand tongues to sing my dear Redeemer's praise," it could be pointed out briefly that Charles Wesley wrote this hymn on the first anniversary of his spiritual birth. Furthermore, the congregation could be asked to observe, while it sings, the blessings of salvation which are mentioned in the hymn.

One of the psychological conditions in the learning process is called "readiness." A congregation can be made ready, even eager, for the joy of singing by an enthusiastic challenge from the leader of worship.

6. *The Leader's Example During Singing*

First a word about rising in time to sing. Simultaneous attack is one of the most important factors in the success of any united endeavor, whether of an army, a football team, or a singing congregation. Certainly a congregation whose members straggle to their feet during the first stanza of a hymn will never have magnificent singing. Their lack of readiness inevitably produces listless singing.

Their leader, obviously, has not instructed them in how to prepare for an attack. There are at least two practices. One is having the congregation stand when the organist plays the first note of the hymn. The congregation further is instructed (and frequently reminded) to use this brief waiting period for three purposes: (1) to catch the rhythm of the tune, (2) to get physically ready for a solid attack in the first syllable, and (3) to glance over the hymn text to gather the main threads of thought.

The more usual custom is to have the congregation stand at the beginning of the last line or phrase of the hymn, if the organist plays the hymn all the way through. Most congregations take their cue for this act of standing from the leader in worship or from the choir. Since some organists abbreviate their introduction to the hymn, it is sometimes difficult to discover just when they will arrive at the last line. Therefore, it is wise perhaps to let the organist nod to the choir at the rising time. The leader and the congregation can thus get the signal from the rising of the choir.

In the opinion of many, it is better to have the people stand for all the hymns in the Sunday morning service. For less formal services, the congregation remains seated during some of the singing.

Now for the example of the leader during singing.

The worship leader should give an enthusiastic example of participation during hymn singing. In most meeting places the pulpit is so situated that the leader is the focus of all eyes as they are raised frequently from the hymnals. If the average worshiper sees a leader who is enthusiastically putting heart and soul into the singing, he is stimulated, ere long, to do likewise. This subtle though powerful pulpit influence on hymn singing cannot be overemphasized.

It must be recognized as fact that not all leaders are endowed equally with singing talent and training. Obviously it would be easy for a minister who has had private voice training and who has sung in a fine college choir to sing comfortably and joyously in front of a congregation. Even the leader who feels that he cannot carry a tune should be encouraged to sing and to offer his praise. There seems to be no justification for the leader's sitting down during hymn singing to look over sermon notes, or for his standing silently surveying the congregation for absentees.

Should a leader desire to save his voice for the message, he ought at least to sing lightly or to read the words while the people are singing. If his throat is slightly sore, he could sing silently, his lips moving but his throat at ease.

This advice to sing enthusiastically should not be construed as a call for boisterous, noisy singing, especially if the leader is near a microphone. During a broadcast the leader should continue singing but either step back several paces from the microphone or request the radio engineer to cut off the pulpit microphone while leaving on the choir pickup.

The minister with a strong voice should not attempt to set the tempo of the hymns. This is the province of the pianist or organist, and any difference of opinion should be resolved in private.

The enthusiastic leadership of a company of Christians gathered to praise their God and Father is a wonderful responsibility. The pastor or shepherd of the flock should lead them in all the experiences of worship, including active participation in hymn singing.

7. The Quotation of Hymns

The custom of quoting lines or stanzas of hymns in prayers, talks, or sermons can be a means of gradually leading our people into a clearer understanding of the ideas in hymns. Of course, the main purpose of quotation is to illumine the idea being presented in the sermon, not to explain the hymn; yet the hymn does become more understandable as a by-product.

In listening to hundreds of excellent sermons and prayers, I have frequently heard snatches of hymns inserted like jewels to sharpen and beautify a thought. "Take from our souls the strain and stress, and let our ordered lives confess the beauty of Thy peace"; "I know not where His islands lift their fronded palms in air; I only know I cannot drift beyond His love and care"; "Love so amazing, so divine, demands my life, my soul, my all"; "Make me a captive, Lord, and then I shall be free"—these and many other quotations have contributed meaning and force.

Paul the preacher loved hymns and quoted them in his Epistles. (See Ephesians 5:14; 1 Timothy 3:16; 2 Timothy 2:11-13.) Bishop Phillips Brooks, the renowned preacher of the last century, had memorized more than two hundred hymns. These lyrics shone like luminous stars through the lines of his sermons.

The point is that many of our greatest hymn writers had the rare gift of turning a phrase so that it expressed spiritual truth with clarity and unusual insight. Occasional and proper quotation of their hymns should assist us in setting forth our thoughts about the Christian faith and life.

Some congregations occasionally read a hymn in unison instead of singing it.

8. Sermons Based on Hymns

Christian sermons are properly based on the Holy Scriptures. Our finest hymns likewise have their roots in God's revealed Word. Since a great deal of Biblical truth is found in certain hymns, some ministers preach sermons or give brief talks from time to time based on these hymn texts. They thereby accomplish two things: first, they illuminate the Scripture passage which gave birth to the lines of the hymn, and, second, they increase the comprehension of the congregation whenever that particular hymn is sung thereafter. It might be suggested, however, that not every hymn found in the average hymnal is a suitable subject for a sermon.

Help in preparing such sermons may be found in Erik Routley's

Hymns and the Faith. This is a collection of interpretive essays on forty-nine familiar hymns.

9. *Hymn Anthems and Responses*

Hymns are primarily considered vehicles for direct congregational expression. They also have considerable worship value when sung as special music by choir, quartet, or soloist, or when played by organist or pianist. Because of the simple structure of a hymn, the congregation can easily grasp the words. Furthermore, a familiar hymn has the advantage of long and tender asssociation in the minds of the people. A worship leader should realize all this and should avail himself of this additional devotional resource.

While objecting to aimless musical elaboration and "enrichment" of services of worship, many leaders believe that the occasional intelligent use of a hymn sung by the choir can be effective. For example, a minister preaching on the need for Christian principles and integrity in government might request the choir to sing Chesterton's stirring hymn, "O God of earth and altar," as the anthem of the morning. To strengthen the impress of a sermon on Christian witness and service, "Lord, speak to me" or "Lead on, O King Eternal" could be requested.

In addition to the occasional use of hymns as anthems, shorter portions can be used as opening choral ascriptions of praise or as responses after Scripture reading, prayer, sermon, or benediction.

As a quiet call to worship some choirs sing the first line and a half of the hymn, "God Himself is with us." For a more joyous choral call to praise, some ministers request the refrain only of "Rejoice, ye pure in heart," or the first stanza of "This is the day the Lord hath made."

As a concluding part of a prayer, the first stanza of "Breathe on me, Breath of God" or the last stanza of "Immortal Love, forever full" or "Prayer is the soul's sincere desire" can be effective. The last line only of "Thou didst leave Thy throne," which reads, "O come to my heart, Lord Jesus: there is room in my heart for Thee!" is an illustration of the use of briefer portions of hymns as prayer responses.

The method of adapting hymns as anthems is dealt with in chapter 10.

Speaking as a choir director, the writer has welcomed occasional requests from worship leaders for special hymn renditions. Choirs naturally need the stimulation of anthems which challenge their technical proficiency, and yet the singers are also willing to tackle the job of presenting a great hymn with utmost skill and reverence.

10. Hymns as Counseling Tools

Thus far we have considered the minister's use of hymns during a service of worship. Not only in the sanctuary but also in the conference room, hymns exercise a healing ministry. As a pastor meets a succession of troubled, questing individuals, he may find opportunity to use a great hymn as a counseling tool.

To one torn by mental anguish, these words from "How firm a foundation" can bring reassurance and calm trust:

> The soul that on Jesus hath leaned for repose,
> I will not, I will not desert to his foes;
> That soul, though all hell should endeavor to shake,
> I'll never, no, never, no, never forsake.

Lines from "Just as I am" can often dissolve the barriers of hesitance in accepting the love and mercy of a Heavenly Father.

To a person troubled by sleepless, fearful nights, a pastor can suggest the quiet repetition of such stanzas as "Give to the winds thy fears; hope and be undismayed" and "Be still, my soul: the Lord is on thy side."

Sometimes it might be a good idea to give this person a little collection of hymns which could be read or sung during the coming days or weeks. I suggest The Wayside Hymnal (Forward Movement). This pocket-sized, paper-backed hymnal contains the words and music of ninety fine hymns.

A shut-in, who would appreciate the solace of hymns, might be lent or given a recording of great hymns. "Praise to the Lord" (Columbia ML 5334) includes hymns sung by the choir of the Church of the Ascension in New York City, Vernon de Tar organist-director. "Songs of Faith" (Decca DL 8039) is a long-playing record of twelve good familiar hymns, sung by the Waring Chapel Choir with Robert Baker at the organ. "A Mighty Fortress" (Victor LM 2199) is sung by the Robert Shaw Chorale.

A prominent Richmond minister quietly entered a hospital room where a lovely young lady lay desperately ill, seemingly unconscious. This pastor spoke just these lines from a familiar hymn, "Be not dismayed whate'er betide, God will take care of you," then slipped out of the room. Some weeks later, this young lady, now on the road to complete recovery, told her pastor that she had heard and understood his reassuring words. They were, she felt, the turning point in her illness.

An unusual and wonderful use of hymns in counseling was recounted by Dr. Joseph R. Sizoo in an article entitled "Kindly Light."[5] During World War II, Dr. Sizoo was a host one evening at a servicemen's canteen in New York City. At a corner booth he found a young British sailor who was deeply disturbed. Sitting down beside him, Dr. Sizoo listened to the sailor's story of the disaster which recently had overwhelmed him.

The lad had been engaged to a British girl in his home town of St. Ives. During a five-day leave they were to be married. Arriving with joyful expectancy at St. Ives, he found to his horror a gaping hole where his fiancee's home had been. The bombers had been over. Her people and his people, and Janie, were gone.

While trying to comfort the lad, Dr. Sizoo discovered that he used to sing in the choir when he was a child. His favorite hymn was "Lead, kindly Light." At Dr. Sizoo's suggestion he began to sing it and his voice became stronger and deeper. Then together far into the night they sang "Abide with me," "O God, our Help in ages past," and many other hymns.

After a long while they arose. Dr. Sizoo, looking into the shining eyes of the lad, asked, "Think you can sleep now?" "Yes, thank you, sir," he replied.

Arm in arm, they walked out into the early morning.

Part Five

THE MUSICAL LEADERSHIP

CHAPTER 9 *The Playing of Hymns*

The hymn player can do more than any other one person to develop great congregational singing. No one else has anything like as much control of the vital processes of hymn singing. The very life of the music flows through his spirit and fingertips.

This truth should constitute a challenge to all church pianists and organists to learn and apply the principles of good hymn playing. The pianist is exceptional and very fortunate whose training in music has included more than a casual reference to congregational accompaniment. Many organists who play Bach and Brahms superbly seem to lack the sympathetic understanding necessary to stimulate congregational singing.

Yet there are definite principles and instructions which, if understood and applied, will go far toward making a first-rate hymn player. These principles, and methods of applying them, will now be discussed. Since pianos are used to accompany hymns more often than are organs, the following remarks are addressed to pianists, with the expectation that organists can readily adapt the instructions to their own instrument. Several paragraphs of hints to organists will conclude this chapter.

1. The Hymn Player Is the Conductor of the Singing

If there is no other person standing in front of the congregation directing with gestures (and there usually is none), the person playing the hymns is the conductor of the singing. The experienced congregational accompanist has discovered that he has almost as much control over the singing of a group of people as if he were standing in front leading. He can indicate from the keyboard the mood and tempo of the music; he can communicate the phrasing and some of the meaning of the text; he can fuse the random impulses of the group by a strong rhythmic leadership at his instrument. He has learned to lead, not follow, the congregation. This does not mean that he races helter-skelter toward the distant goal—the Amen—with a few energetic members of the congregation hanging on desperately. It does mean that he exercises control and that he uses this control with understanding.

Perhaps a reference to two different meanings of accompaniment will clarify the matter. A person is a good accompanist of a solo singer or instrumentalist when the accompanying instrument is subordinate, when the solo melody is clearly set forth. Such a definition presupposes a soloist with musical artistry, one who knows just how fast or slow to sing at a given spot in the song, how loud or soft, just how long to pause between sections of the music.

But a congregation has no strong musical will; it does not know at what speed to sing or how to change volume effectively. Like a flock of sheep, it needs to be led. The pianist playing for a congregation, therefore, has an entirely different problem. Unlike the accompanist of the soloist, he must conduct and lead the singing.

This fact immediately demands a change of attitude on the part of many timid young players who have meekly let the congregation or young people's group have its own musical way. They must decide to become masters of the singing, determining what tempo and expression are to be used. Then with a firm, solid touch at the keyboard they must strive constantly to control and mold the singing of the people.

Speaking of keyboard touch, here is a practical suggestion. Many pianos lack the sonority and magnitude of tone to supply adequate volume for leading a large assembly. Rather than bang noisily on the keys, many pianists double (add a lower octave to) the bass notes on many chords. This gives additional depth and weight to the piano tone, much as the addition of the pedal stops reinforces the organ tone. A little experience will teach the be-

ginner how to fill out the chord with the right hand, the tenor
notes being taken usually by the right thumb.

This advice about adding bass notes should be safeguarded by
urging the beginner first to learn to play the hymns exactly as
written in the four voice parts. Such preliminary practice will
prevent the changing of chords and the muddying of texture when
the bass is doubled. For accompanying small groups of worshipers
and choirs, the four-voice parts of the hymn without any doubling
furnish a sufficient body of tone. Most good hymn pianists feel
that playing the right hand an octave higher is not a good general
practice.

Always be sure to strike both hands simultaneously. Seesawing
at the keyboard is unforgivable. "Let him that thinketh he stand-
eth take heed lest he fall."

2. The Pianist Calls Attention to the Hymn, Not to Self

The hymn is the thing, not the pianist. The hymn has a spiritual
message for the worshipers. The pianist, therefore, should strive
to eliminate everything which would distract the worshiper from
God and attract him toward the person at the keyboard.

Wrong notes which spoil the harmony and grate on the ear,
long rolling chords or arpeggios, dazzling glissandos which demon-
strate the player's technique but do not point to God, hymns
played so fast that the people cannot catch sufficient breath or
played so slowly that the people are exhausted—these are some
things which distract a congregation from true worship. In
suggesting that these distractions be weeded out, we do not
recommend characterless playing, but hymn accompaniment which

THE HYMN AND CONGREGATIONAL SINGING

is entirely unselfish, leading always to the experience of worship through music.

3. The Hymn Player Is Consistent

Consistency will aid the hymn player at every turn, whereas lack of it will get him into endless trouble. Few other attributes are more appreciated by a congregation, because the members soon learn that they can trust the consistent pianist not to let them down, or to embarrass them by some unusual temperamental turn in the playing. Members of a congregation have the right to expect, for example, that the pianist will afford them approximately the same interval of time between all stanzas, that the pianist will not speed up on one stanza and drag out the next, that the pianist will give them sufficient leadership on both syllables of the Amen, that the pianist will not scare them with a quiet passage after a loud phrase.

This right of the congregation to expect consistency in its accompanist is immediately asserted when some unusual trick is indulged in by the pianist. The man in the pew simply shuts up. He is not going to be caught out on a musical limb. None of us wants to sound out at the wrong time above the crowd.

A consistent hymn player, then, is one who understands the viewpoint of the singer in the pew and is one who plays in such a way that this member of the congregation always knows what to expect.

4. The Hymn Player Is Accurate

Accuracy is the foundation stone of music; without it we are on shifting sands. Conductors of great orchestras and virtuosos are sticklers for accuracy. Perfectionists, we call them. Congregations which listen during the week to their music on the radio and TV and in concert hall cannot help noticing errors in hymn playing on Sunday. Therefore church musicians must strive constantly for complete accuracy, securing the hymn numbers before the service and diligently practicing the tunes until they are perfectly mastered.

There are two types of accuracy for which we should strive: (1)

accuracy of pitch interval and (2) accuracy of time. The first of
these is more readily achieved, because it is the more obvious of
the two types. Even the musically untutored layman winces at a
discord or a flatted tone. Accuracy of interval has to do with the
correct pitch. By learning to read the correct note meticulously,
by looking ahead of the spot at which one is at the moment playing, and especially by remembering the influence throughout the
tune of each sharp or flat in the key signature, most of the dis-
cords and inaccuracies can be eliminated. Occasionally a chord
will have more than an octave in the left hand. In this case, the
right hand includes the tenor note in its grasp, thus in "Welcome,
happy morning":

Accuracy of time value is even more essential, and yet it is the
rarer of the two. Many pianists who shudder at a discord in their
playing distort time values beyond recognition. To play time
values accurately is important because it contributes directly to
the rhythm or life pulse of the music. Accurate time is the basis
of good rhythm.

Here are three common errors in time values:

a. *Failure to sustain long notes and to pull through dotted
notes.* A dotted half note becomes a half note in many tunes like
St. Catherine ("Faith of our fathers," P348; "O Jesus Christ, our
Lord most dear," E185), Hursley ("Sun of my soul," P56, E166),
Finlandia ("Be still, my soul," P374), and Italian Hymn, some-
times called Moscow ("Come, Thou Almighty King," P244,
E271).

Clipping time from a note usually means starting the next note
prematurely and thus distorting the rhythm. In sustaining a long
note in a hymn tune, the beat of the pulse should be felt by the

pianist. Notice the dotted whole note in this phrase[1] from "All creatures of our God and King":

The habit of thinking of all long notes as being made up of several shorter notes tied together is most useful in developing sustained tone of proper length. For example:

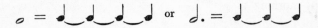

b. *Tendency to clip rests.* Some players tend to ignore rests in four-four tunes like AR HYD Y NOS ("God, that madest earth and heaven," P58). Hymn players should feel the pulse beat of the music right through the silences.

c. *Tendency to hurry eighth notes.* The first phrase of the melody from ST. MARGARET ("O Love that wilt not let me go," P400, E458) can trip up many pianists who fail to grasp the relationship between the quarter and eighth notes. As a British writer says, "The average singer [or pianist] gets too much pace on whenever the notes show tails."[2] For other examples, see SERENITY ("Immortal Love, forever full," P229), LUX BENIGNA ("Lead, kindly Light," P331, E430), WHAT A FRIEND ("What a Friend we have in Jesus," P385, E422), ANTIOCH ("Joy to the world," P161).

The pianist finds the remedy who "counts the time," who visualizes—or actually marks—the pulse beats above the score of each hymn, and who strives to maintain within himself the rhythmic stride of the music.

Metronomes. Frequent practice with a metronome, first slow, then progressively faster, will be an excellent aid in developing this accurate pulsation.

Fermatas. This little symbol (⌢) is found in many hymnals at the end of phrases in tunes such as ST. ANNE ("O God, our Help"), EIN' FESTE BURG ("A mighty Fortress"), and CANONBURY ("Lord, speak to me"). Many organists treat this as a sign to prolong the note. More frequently it should be treated simply as a signal to take a breath and move on. *The Hymnal* 1940 (Episcopal) has handled this matter by eliminating all fermatas and writing in the exact time values of phrase terminals.

5. The Hymn Player Is Rhythmical

A player who has learned to play the time values of hymn tunes exactly as written has taken a long step toward rhythmic playing. No accurate time values, no dynamic rhythm! But rhythm is more than a matter of time values. It is more than a steady succession of strong beats followed by one or more weak pulses. This definition of rhythm has been accepted by so many people for so long that we had better pause for a moment and consider it.

Musicians dealing with the hymn tune form are tempted to accept it unquestioningly, for the hymn tune seems to illustrate exactly the regular pattern of strong and weak beats. The hymn tune, after all, must be simple enough to carry the slowest amateurs of the congregation; consequently, most tunes have strong accentual pegs at the beginning of each measure for the mass of wayward singers to grab. In three-four tunes like KREMSER ("We gather together," P18, E315) and ITALIAN HYMN ("Come, Thou Almighty King," P244, E271) we have a strong beat followed by two weak beats. In four-four tunes like LANCASHIRE ("Lead on, O King Eternal," P332, E257), NICAEA ("Holy, Holy, Holy! Lord God Almighty," P11, E266), and AURELIA ("The Church's one Foundation," P437, E396) each measure begins with a primary pulse accent and on the third beat each has a secondary accent.

Recognition of this structural fact may be sufficient for many pianists. But for great hymn playing we must think further into the meaning of rhythm.

The good definition of rhythm, applying to hymn playing, which

has come to my attention is by a Scottish musician, Willan Swain-
son of Aberdeen, who says: "Musical rhythm is a sense of vitality,
progression, and balance produced by the influence of duration,
speed, and accent upon pitch."[3]

These words are carefully chosen and it will repay the reader to
study them and to return to them after reading this discussion.

Now, many pianists who attempt to be rhythmic in their playing greatly overwork variation in tempo (*tempo rubato*). Such
pianists underwork variation in accent. A pianist who understands
the different types of accent will rarely have to resort to more than
a minute variation of tempo. His playing of hymns will manifest
that sense of vitality, progression, and balance which is rhythm.

Five Types of Accent. From the types of accent defined in
Grove's Dictionary of Music and Musicians, fifth edition (see
article "TIME: Accent"), we list the following as being important
in the playing of hymn tunes:

(1) *Metric accent* is the importance given to the first note in
each measure. We have discussed this above, briefly. It is the most
common and most overworked type of accent, certainly among
hymn players. All too often there is such a relentless clubbing of
the first note in the measure that the other subtler forms of accent
are quite neglected. Metric accent, however, has its values, and
should be tastefully used, because it is the device for securing unity
in the tune. The correlative of unity—which is variety—is gained
by the use of the types of accent which follow.

(2) *Agogic accent* is the importance given to the longer of two
successive notes. Other factors being equal, a note twice or three
times as long gives to its accompanying syllable a tendency to
emphasis. The hymn, "Jesus, Thou Joy of loving hearts," among
many possible examples, illustrates agogic accent in simple form.
The tune gives twice the time to the italicized syllables, and
thus helps to bring out the meaning of the text.

> Jesus, Thou *Joy* of *loving hearts,*
>   Thou Fount of *life,* Thou *Light* of *men,*
> From the best *bliss* that *earth* im*parts*
>   We turn un*filled* to *Thee* again.

Of course, other forms of accent are also present in the music and are influencing the text. What are they?

(3) *Tonic, or pitch, accent* is the emphasis which a high note tends to have. Illustrations of this are apparent in any hymn tune.

(4) *Dynamic or stress accent* is the importance given a certain note of the melody by the application of tonal force; in other words, by increased volume. In good hymns most of the accented syllables coincide with the strong beats of the music, as in the first stanza of "O God, our Help in ages past." Look, however, at the first measure of the five stanzas of "Jesus, Thou Joy of loving hearts." The speech accent falls not on the first but on the second syllable in the last four stanzas:

> Stanza 1. Jesus, Thou Joy . . .
> Stanza 2. Thy *truth* unchanged . . .
> Stanza 3. We *taste* Thee . . .
> Stanza 4. Our *restless* spirits . . .
> Stanza 5. O Jesus, ever . . .

This discrepancy between the metric (first in the measure) accent and the normal emphasis of intelligent reading can be offset by the pianist who applies a slight dynamic or stress accent to the second note of the first measure when stanzas 2-5 are being sung. This example shows how dynamic accent can make for intelligent singing, especially since syllabic accents vary greatly from stanza to stanza.

For the sake of practice, it might be helpful in a few hymns to underline the accented syllables in all stanzas before playing them in a service. In such congregational accompaniment, however, be sure to give a sufficient amount of the unifying metric accent.

(5) *Cumulative accent* falls upon a note when the preceding notes are arranged in such a way as to give it emphasis.

The last phrase from the tune DARWELL'S 148TH ("Rejoice, the Lord is King," P140, E600) shows how the melody has been arranged to throw an inevitable emphasis on the high D.

The third phrase of the tune LYONS ("O worship the King," P26) illustrates the same thing. The first two phrases of the familiar Doxology tune, OLD HUNDREDTH, get off with much more of a rhythmic spring as the reiterated G's and B's produce a mild cumulative accent on the second note of each phrase. In Goss's tune, BENEDIC ANIMA MEA ("Praise, my soul, the King of heaven," P31, E282), the four A's give quite an accumulation of rhythmic accent to the first high D.

A careful study and use of these five kinds of accent in many hymns will enable an organist or pianist to unfold the rhythmic nature of the music in a beautiful and compelling way.

The word rhythm is derived from the Greek verb "rhein," which means "to flow." How apt a derivation, for the basis of all music is tonal movement.

An excellent pianist, for example, does not move from chord to chord of the great Irish tune, ST. COLUMBA ("The King of love my Shepherd is," P106, E345), in picket-fence fashion, but rather moves through these chords and along the melody to certain chosen points of climax and repose.

His music flows. In order to know where to move in a tune, the pianist should know the architecture of the hymn tunes and the shape of phrases within these tunes.

6. *The Hymn Player Follows the Text*

The most important part of a hymn is the text. Certainly it is essential to read the entire texts of the hymns to be played the next Sunday.

The pianist who tries to bring out the meaning of the text by careful phrasing finds it comparatively easy to do so in well-wrought hymns like "Hark, the herald angels sing," "Lead on, O King Eternal," and "Joyful, joyful, we adore Thee." In these hymns the textual and musical phrases coincide at almost every point.

The problem of intelligent phrasing becomes complex, however, in the many hymns in which the musical phrase ends in the middle of a thought group, between subject and verb, or between verb and direct object. In the following examples the musical phrase arrives at its point of momentary repose at the end of each line. Here the congregation takes a breath ordinarily. The thought, however, is completed in the next line, and unless careful concentration is maintained, most of the singers will have the thread of thought snatched from them by this interruptive act of breath taking.

> He makes me down to lie
> In pastures green; He leadeth me
> The quiet waters by.[4]

> When the sun of bliss is beaming
> Light and love upon my way.[5]

What is to be done with spots like these? Dr. Percy Scholes points out that singing is a compromise between text and tune.[6] Some pianists, by keyboard example and by verbal precept, can teach a choir and, rarely, a congregation, to carry over the end of a musical phrase without a breath and thus not to break the textual phrase. Such effort, however, is often costly. The singers virtuously span the end of the musical phrase, but, out of breath, they frequently must collect a breath before reaching their destination—the period, semicolon, or comma. It should not be inferred that it is not possible frequently to accomplish this adjustment of a musical and a textual phrase. However, unless it is easy to sing a complete verbal phrase with one supply of breath and unless the majority of the congregation comprehend the scheme, it seems better to take a breath at the end of each line

and to try to keep the thought sequence unbroken in the minds
of the singers.

Punctuation marks in hymns, we have seen, cause much trouble.
It is a mistake to believe that every comma means a breath or a
break in time. There are two kinds of commas, one of which
implies a breath, the other of which is observed by a slight leaning
on the preceding syllable. The comma in "Be still, my soul: the
Lord is on thy side" obviously does not indicate a breath or a
break after "still." To chop up the first line of "Holy, Holy, Holy!
Lord God Almighty!" and "Praise ye the Lord, the Almighty, the
King of creation!" is inexcusable. Generally speaking, no mark of
punctuation should cause a break in the movement of a hymn
except at the ends of musical phrases and lines. The last lines of
"O worship the King" and "How firm a foundation" are two
notable exceptions.

A hymn player who pays attention to these instructions will per-
force have to keep his eyes on the text of all stanzas. He must
always play the words as well as the music.

A pianist should also sing (quietly, lest he be unable to hear the
congregation) in order that he may breathe sympathetically with
those whom he accompanies. By so doing, he is more apt to
allow just the right amount of time for the various breaths needed
in the hymn.

7. *The Hymn Player Uses the Right Tempo*

The use of the correct tempo is probably the most important
single aspect of good hymn playing. A common criticism of a
person's hymn accompaniment is that "he played too fast" or "she
dragged the tempo."

John Wesley concludes one of his "Directions for Singing"
(see chapter 3) with this caution: "and take care not to sing too
slow. This drawling way naturally steals on all who are lazy; and
it is high time to drive it out from among us, and sing all our
tunes just as quick as we did at first." Many of us pianists and
organists are apt to err on the slow side.

The best way to determine the correct tempo for singing a particular hymn is to approach the subject with no prejudice toward

either fast, slow, or medium speed. Hymns have different paces, and to play them all at a rapid or slow speed is unwise. Here are some ways of discovering the correct tempo:

(1) Identify the mood of the text and tune. Some hymnals (*The Hymnal*, 1933, Presbyterian, USA, and *The Hymnal* 1940, Episcopal) wisely indicate this predominant feeling by placing at the head of each hymn a phrase like one of these: "Majestically," "In flowing style," "With joy," "With quiet dignity," "Slow, with serenity." Reading the text aloud with such a feeling helps to define the tempo.

(2) Study the structure of the tune. Some tunes with flippant rhythmic patterns can be ennobled by a broader, more dignified treatment. Tunes with longer phrases usually should move along more briskly than hymns with abbreviated phrases; otherwise, people will be snatching breaths all along the line.

Broad, dignified tunes like St. Anne ("O God, our Help"), Ein' Feste Burg ("A mighty Fortress is our God"), Dundee ("O God of Bethel, by whose hand"), and St. Peter ("In Christ there is no East or West"), which change harmonies on almost every chord and which use the root position of many of these chords, require an unhurried, more majestic tempo. We can safely feel a slight impulse on each of these chords.

On the other hand, tunes like St. Gertrude ("Onward, Christian soldiers") and Aurelia ("The Church's one Foundation") change harmonies less frequently and can be carried along with more dispatch. In this second type of tune, a compelling forward stride will be given the rhythm if we feel an impulse on the first and third beats of each measure, in which case the 4/4 time becomes 2/2 time (*alla breve*). See Truro ("Lift up our hearts, O King of Kings," P481) and Duke Street ("O Lord, Thou art my God and King," P5), which have the 2/2 time signature.

(c) Consider external factors such as acoustics and age of singers. Contrast a festive morning service with a quiet evensong, a convention of youth with a congregation of older Christians, a small prayer meeting with a vast assemblage, a compact chapel with a reverberating cathedral. These external factors condition our decision as to a proper pace but do not necessarily indicate a snail speed for the latter situations.

(d) Observe the tempos at which other pianists and organists play similar hymns. We can learn from others, but we must not forget that we are all different in our emotional and musical makeup and thus that we can rarely agree on the precise tempo for a particular tune. After a certain morning service two visiting organists commented on my playing of the Doxology. One thought it was too slow; the other deemed it a trifle fast!

Below are the metronomic indications for a number of representative tunes as the writer would usually play them. There are dangers in presenting such tempos, yet we should not be indefinite in treating this subject.

(Q means Quarter Note, H means Half-Note)

AUSTRIAN HYMN ("Glorious things of thee are spoken") H 54–58
CREATION ("The spacious firmament on high") .... H 66 –72
EIN' FESTE BURG ("A mighty Fortress is our God") .. Q 80 –88
HYMN TO JOY ("Joyful, joyful, we adore Thee") .... H 60 –66
ITALIAN HYMN ("Come, Thou Almighty King") .... Q 108–116
LYONS ("O worship the King") .... Q 108–116
MARTYN ("Jesus, Lover of my soul") ...... dotted H 48 –52
NICAEA ("Holy, Holy, Holy! Lord God Almighty!") . Q 104–112
OLD HUNDREDTH ("Praise God from whom all blessings flow") .... Q 84 –92
QUEBEC ("Jesus, Thou Joy of loving hearts") .... Q 96 –104
ST. ANNE ("O God, our Help in ages past") .... Q 69 –76
TERRA BEATA ("This is my Father's world") .... H 54 –58

8. The Hymn Player in the Worship Service

Before touching the keyboard, mentally feel the tempo and rhythmic pattern of the tune to be played. If necessary, tap out a measure or so with your finger. For instance, before playing "Ancient of Days" tap out the rhythm of the first phrase.

If the congregation knows the tune, why play it over before singing it? There are a number of reasons why at least a portion should be played over. Here are some of them.

(1) The congregation, consciously or unconsciously, senses the mood of the piece from the way it is rendered at the keyboard. Pianists, consequently, should strive to communicate the feeling of the tune, whether it be a mood of joy, majesty, or pensiveness. This playing-over is an emotional prelude to the singing.

(2) The congregation learns the pace or tempo at which the hymn is to be sung. Since this is so, the pianist should play over the tune with clear, incisive touch at exactly the same tempo at which the congregation is expected to sing. Some pianists prefer to play over the tune faster than the people are expected to sing. To me this seems inconsistent. A congregation can be trained, by verbal announcement or by a note in the bulletin, to listen to the tempo announced by the instrument and then to sing at the same rate of speed. In this connection, you might use in the Sunday bulletin John Wesley's "Directions" concerning pace in singing. (See chapter 3.)

(3) The congregation learns the pitch. It also has opportunity to find the place in the hymnal and to rise with the choir and minister—usually at the beginning of the last line—in time to sing the first note together.

In the formal Sunday morning service of many churches the entire tune is played through, except where the people may already be standing at the announcement of the hymn—for example, after a responsive reading. Then a phrase or line is sufficient. At less formal services where a number of hymns are sung, it saves time to play only a part of the tune. Only let that portion of the hymn be musically complete with a well-rounded cadence. If the tune is abbreviated in playing over, be sure to have an understanding with choir and minister as to the moment they are to stand. Do not retard at the end of this playing.

Having played the tune over, in entirety or in part, the pianist is ready for a good clean start with the congregation. The people will learn to come together with him for a solid attack on the first note if he establishes a definite length of time between all stanzas and consistently sticks to it. There should be no variation in this interval, even if the hymnal has to be adjusted, organ stops added, or a signal given the singers to stand.

Allow enough time at the end of stanzas for a comfortable breath by the congregation. This normal "refueling" of breath is well-nigh impossible if the pianist observes precisely the time value of the last note and moves relentlessly into the next stanza. Yet some pianists consistently do this.

There should be little, preferably no retard at the end of any stanza except the last. Keep the tempo up, otherwise inertia— ever present in a congregation—will assert itself in a marked slowing down at the end of the first stanza. When the second stanza begins, it is difficult to recapture the initial vitality of rhythm. It is better to reserve the retard for the last few notes of the last phrase of the final stanza. Then the singers will respond to a broadening of tempo and reach an inspiring climax.

An Amen is an integral part of a hymn and thus it should reflect the character and mood of the hymn. If the tune is majestic, the Amen should be sounded with equal loftiness and confidence. A more reflective hymn needs a quieter, but vital Amen. We should do away with the type of devitalized Amens heard in so many of our churches. The main reason why it is sung so weakly (or not sung at all) is that the congregational support has been removed by so much reduction of piano or organ tone. The man in the pew therefore feels quite uncertain about just when each syllable of the Amen is to be uttered and so he does not sing at all. Firm leadership at the keyboard and some verbal reassurance and instruction of the congregation can overcome this practice.

As some pianists approach the two chords of the Amen, they strike the bass note of the first chord before the other parts of the chord are sounded. This preliminary bridge note reassures the members of the congregation that the Amen is to follow and it helps them to time their entrance upon it.

Except for festival procession hymns, it is preferable to eliminate interludes between stanzas.[7]

Lower keys. Several leading hymnals, such as *The Hymnal* 1940 (Episcopal) and *The Hymnbook* (Presbyterian 1955), have many tunes in lower keys. If the hymns in other books are pitched too high, and if the organist or pianist cannot transpose with accuracy, then the musician might purchase one of these two books and keep it at the instrument for use when lower keys are needed.

9. *Specific Suggestions to Organists*

Volume. Use proper volume for size of congregation and type of hymn. The accompaniment should have sufficient fullness to produce confidence in singers. Avoid oppressive loudness. The congregation will respond readily to firm, rhythmical playing at moderate volume. Occasionally request the opinion of several intelligent members of the congregation regarding the volume of your playing.

Do not surprise the congregation by changing volume too abruptly and too frequently. It is quite proper within limits to vary volume from stanza to stanza (see, for example, the third and fourth stanzas of "When I survey the wondrous cross"), but do not try to interpret every shade of meaning in the text. Generally speaking, be conservative in your changes of dynamics.

Registration. Discover the clearest ensemble available on your instrument.[8] Your battle is partially won if your organ has a properly designed diapason chorus. Use sufficient 8-foot stops to define the pitch line but add a generous number of 4-, 2 2/3-, and 2-foot stops. On some smaller instruments the Swell to Great 4-foot coupler helps to give a clear texture to the tone. Avoid any 16-foot manual stops and in hymn playing always leave off 16-foot manual couplers. Few things can muddy accompaniment so rapidly.

If the organ is inadequate, then most of the stops must be drawn to supply sufficient volume. However, most organs have sufficient size to permit some judicious alteration of quality for special effects. For example, a predominantly reed tone can accentuate a vigorous stanza. Infrequently the melody may be taken firmly by a solo stop with accompaniment on another manual. For the accompaniment of congregational singing, avoid sugary, ear-tickling combinations and the use of tremulants and celestes.

Do not use the pedals all the time. Occasionally during the playing over and during a quieter stanza (or part of a stanza) drop the pedals out. Their re-entry is all the more effective after their absence.

Touch. Good organ instruction books usually have advice regarding hymn playing. See, for example, Gleason's *Method of Organ*

Playing and Peeters' *Little Organ Book.* Maintain a happy balance between the use of staccato (separated or detached) and legato (connected) touch, using more of the former to establish an incisive rhythm, using more of the latter when congregational momentum has been established. At no time should your playing sound choppy.

Breath pauses. It is a good practice to lift the hands at the ends of musical phrases, especially at the conclusion of those which coincide with the end of thought phrases. This valuable habit enables the singers to know where to breathe. Likewise, if the organist will give a brief period of silence between the final chord of one stanza and the initial chord of the next, the congregation will know confidently when to attack the next stanza. This breath pause should be of consistent length from stanza to stanza.

Amens. We have already discussed playing Amens on the piano. Now for Amens played on the organ. There is one tone in the final chord of the hymn which also occurs in the first chord of the Amen. Many organists hold this tone as a kind of bridge between hymn and Amen. It seems to reassure the people that the Amen is forthcoming and it enables them to prepare their breath. As a rule the organ tone should not be reduced.

Electronic organs and hymn playing. Brief advice is difficult. Too much volume should be avoided, especially if the tone chamber is directed toward the congregation and not toward the organist. Use as clear an ensemble as you can register. Secure congregational motion by sprightly touch rather than by a torrent of tone. Be careful not to draw on too much pedal tone. Do not use tremulants.

Varied hymn accompaniments and preludes. The spiritual effectiveness of hymns depends on the maintenance of reverent attention throughout the singing. One reason the interest frequently flags is the unvaried repetition of the same music for four to six stanzas. The text constantly presents new ideas but the music remains the same.

Enterprising hymn players, therefore, occasionally vary the accompaniment to hymn tunes. It is a spiritually thrilling experience to be part of a large congregation singing a familiar hymn when on an appropriate stanza a new lift is given by varied skill-ful harmonization at the organ. Since most organists do not possess the ability to improvise appropriate inspiring harmonies to a hymn melody, it is fortunate that some excellent collections are available. Here are several:

Eric Thiman, *Varied Accompaniments to Thirty-four Well-known Tunes for Unison Singing.* (Oxford.)
> Dr. Thiman's settings of AURELIA ("The Church's one Foundation"), OLD HUNDREDTH ("The Doxology"), and ST. COLUMBA ("The King of love my Shepherd is") are superb.

Eric Thiman, *Varied Harmonizations of Favorite Hymn Tunes for Organ.* (H. W. Gray.)

T. Tertius Noble, *Free Organ Accompaniments to One Hundred Well-known Hymn Tunes.* (J. Fischer and Bro.)
> Dr. Noble's harmonizations of NICAEA ("Holy, Holy, Holy"), ST. GERTRUDE ("Onward, Christian soldiers"), and EVENTIDE ("Abide with me") are among his best.

Edward C. Bairstow, *Organ Accompaniments to the Unison Verses of 24 Hymn Tunes from The English Hymnal.* (Oxford.)
> Sir Edward Bairstow's arrangements of PICARDY ("Let all mortal flesh") and EBENEZER ("Once to every man and na-tion") are particularly good.

Henry Coleman, *Varied Hymn Accompaniments.* (Oxford.)

Dr. Thiman, incidentally, has a short practical treatise on methods of improvising one's own varied harmonies. It is called *Varied Harmonies to Hymn Tunes* (Oxford).

Three bits of advice might be given about the use of these varied or "free" hymn accompaniments.

First, they should not be overused. To climax a festival morn-ing hymn, to add quiet interest in an evening prayer hymn, or to increase brilliance in an Easter or Christmas hymn of praise—these are some of the proper occasional uses.

Second, when the organist is playing a varied accompaniment to a stanza, the choir and congregation are expected, of course, to sing a strong unison melody.

Third, it is usually a good idea to tell the congregation, in writing or verbally, what a varied organ hymn accompaniment is, why it is being used, and how the people should sing when the accompaniment is being played.

Hymn Preludes. A very complete list of hymn tune preludes is found in *The Hymnal 1940 Companion* (Episcopal), pages 609-680.[9]

Among the scores of available collections might be mentioned the following:

Bingham, *Twelve Hymn Preludes,* Sets 1, 2. (H. W. Gray.)

Bingham, *Seven Preludes on Lowell Mason Hymns.* (H. W. Gray.)

Coleman, *Ten Hymn Tune Voluntaries* (2 vols.). (Stainer and Bell.)

Vaughan Williams, *Three Chorale Preludes.* (Stainer and Bell.)

Pfatteicher and Davison, *The Church Organist's Golden Treasury,* Vols. 1-2. (Ditson.)

Sowerby, *Meditations on Communion Hymns.* (H. W. Gray.)

Willan, *Ten Hymn Preludes* (Sets I, II). (Peters.)

Eighty Chorale Preludes (Ed. by Keller). (Peters.)

Reger, *Thirty Short Chorale Preludes.* (Peters.)

CHAPTER **10** The Choirs and
Hymn Singing

The choirs are committees of the congregation charged with responsibility for the music of the service of worship. Although the singing of anthems and "special" music is important, the prime responsibility of the choirs is the leadership of congregational singing.

The choirs, after all, are composed of people who are more confident of their singing ability. Frequently they read musical notation reasonably well. They enjoy singing. They have opportunity for regular instruction. For these reasons, they are musical shepherds of the flock.

Here are several ways they can help.

1. Members of the choirs should give an enthusiastic example of participation in the singing. By their facial and vocal expression they can stimulate the people of the pews to imitate them. The choir members are frequently in full view of the congregation, and the earnest attention and interest of the choristers will be readily apparent.

2. They can encourage the congregation to sing by expressing interest and encouragement when they mingle with the congregation in the ordinary walks of life. Most of the choristers have families out in the pews and it helps for a more expert singer to commend a layman on an honest attempt at singing a new hymn.

3. Many children's choirs have hymn study projects. Notebooks devoted to hymn stories and pictures are constructed. Quizzes of hymn facts are given. The educational values of these projects feed into the leadership given by the children's choirs.

4. The choirs can teach an unfamiliar hymn. Since the choirs can rehearse and master a new tune, the members are quite able to outline the melody and guide the people as they attempt the unfamiliar hymn. One of the best ways is to have all the choir singers sing only the melody, at least on the first and last stanzas, preferably on all stanzas. The melody is the path which most of the congregation will try to traverse, and if it is boldly delineated by all the choristers, then the congregation will be reassured and helped.

5. The choirs can teach a new hymn by singing it as an anthem. Hymns, when arranged skillfully, make beautiful and impressive anthems. What is more, they constitute an economical source of special choral music, for the material is instantly available in any good hymnal. In suggesting that hymns be used as anthems, the writer does not mean to recommend their exclusive use, of course. There are too many lovely anthems which should not be neglected.

The secret lies in arranging the hymns in interesting, varied ways so as to bring out the beauties inherent in the harmony and melody and in order to interpret effectively the meaning of the text. For the average choir to sing all five stanzas of a hymn in straight four-part harmony would be monotonous, to say the least.

Ways of varying the singing of hymn stanzas. Here, first, is a list of twelve ways of varying the singing of certain stanzas of hymns and then, second, are three examples of hymns arranged in some of these special ways.

(1) All voices singing full harmony (accompanied or unaccompanied).

(2) All voices singing melody (unison).

(3) Men singing melody alone.

(4) Women singing melody alone.

(5) Solo voice singing melody accompanied by choir humming regular harmonies. If no soloist is available, have the entire section become a solo section, striving for clear blended tones.

(6) Altos, tenors, and basses singing melody, with sopranos singing a descant. See the descants in *The Hymnbook* (Presbyterian 1955) of hymns 11 (NICAEA), 40 (NEANDER), 510 (MATERNA). Also you might order a good descant collection.

Descants to 31 Well-Known Hymn Tunes, by David McK. Williams (The H. W. Gray Co.) is a good one. (See also *20 Hymn-Tune Descants* by C. S. Lang and *The Descant Hymn-Tune Book* by G. Shaw, both published by Novello.)

(7) Sopranos and tenors singing their parts as a duet if these two voice parts are harmoniously arranged. (See, for example, ST. COLUMBA P106.)

(8) Men singing the melody, altos their own part, and sopranos singing the tenor part an octave higher.

(9) A quartet, trio, or duet of solo voices.

(10) A solo voice or section singing the melody with varied harmonization of accompaniment. *The Hymnbook* (Presbyterian 1955) has two different and effective means of alternate hymn tune harmonizations:

Instrumental alternate accompaniments are found for two tunes: LAUDA ANIMA (31) and AURELIA (437). Collections containing other alternate harmonizations have been listed in chapter 9.

Choral alternate harmonizations with melody in the tenor are provided for five tunes in this same Presbyterian *Hymnbook*: DUNDEE (112), OLD HUNDREDTH (24), ST. BRIDE (308), ST. MAGNUS (211), and SOUTHWELL (270). See Healey Willan's *Faux-Bourdons and New Hymn Tunes,* a collection of sixteen alternate choral harmonizations to well-known hymn tunes (Western Music Company).

(11) One or more stanzas sung in parts by men alone or women alone.

For women's voices, *A Book of Chorales* by Bach-Geer (Concordia) is a good sample.

Here are two collections of hymns for male voices: *Hymnal and Service Book for Male Voices* (Summy) and *Hymns of Faith,* edited by Wismar (Concordia).

(12) Modulation to a higher or lower key.

Now let us take three examples of hymns arranged in some of these special ways.

(1) "Once to every man and nation." EBENEZER (TON-Y-BOTEL) P361, E519. Half note at about 80 metronome. Here is one way of arranging the stanzas:

Stanza 1. Straight four-part harmony sung throughout by all voices.

Stanza 2. All men singing the melody, altos singing their regular part, and sopranos singing the tenor an octave higher. A very effective arrangement. (Suggested under No. 8 above.)

Stanza 3. First two lines sung in full harmony. On last two lines all voices sing in unison to make a strong climax.

(2) "All creatures of our God and King." LASST UNS ERFREUEN P100. Half note at about 76. There are many possibilities for variation in treatment. Instead of outlining an arrangement for all stanzas, a number of ways of varying a single stanza are indicated. Don't try them all in any one stanza when you sing the hymn!

Line 1: All voices singing whole line in unison. Conceivably, an echo effect could be secured even this soon in the piece by having the men or women sing the first half of the line with the opposite section of the choir responding.

Line 2: A more logical spot for antiphonal effect. Should be sung in harmony as contrast to the unison of line 1. The second "Alleluia" as an echo could be sung by a quartet either in the choir loft or in the balcony of the church. The latter part of line 2 and most of line 3 might be taken by a strong, clear solo voice or by the sopranos alone.

Line 3 (last two measures) and Line 4: "O praise Him" in harmony with the second one sung by reduced choir or by echo quartet. The second "Alleluia" also sung in echo fashion. Last "Alleluia" to be sung by all voices in harmony or unison. (Be sure to give three full beats to next to last measure.)

(3) "Thou hidden Source of calm repose." ST. PETERSBURG P423. Quarter note at 108 to 120. This great Russian tune is published in several anthem forms. A good one is "Thy wisdom, Lord," arranged by A. T. Davison (E. C. Schirmer).

Stanza 1. Full choir in four-part harmony.

Stanza 2. Alto and soprano duet accompanied either by instrument or by rest of choir humming quietly.

Stanza 3. Quartet in harmony.

Stanza 4. All voices in unison. Amen in harmony.

These three examples illustrate how hymns can be arranged simply and effectively as anthems.

Listed below are a number of tunes from *The Hymnbook* (Presbyterian 1955) which would make beautiful anthems. Try your hand at arranging them and your choir at singing them. Do not make the arrangements too fancy, and be sure that your choir members know the plan exactly.

ARFON (197), INNSBRUCK (66), BOUNDLESS MERCY (39), JESU, MEINE FREUDE (414), BRYN CALFARIA (90), KING'S WESTON (143), BUNESSAN (464), KINGSFOLD (177), CHRISTE SANCTORUM (43), LLANGLOFFAN (231), DURROW (93), MOVILLE (136), ES IST EIN ROS' (162), O GOTT, DU FROMMER GOTT (128), FINGAL (321), SINE NOMINE (425), FOREST GREEN (96), VOM HIMMEL HOCH (173), HERZLIEBSTER JESU (191), WALSALL (129), HIGH ROAD (22).

Here are several hymn-anthems from among hundreds which could be suggested:

PICARDY. Holst. "Let all mortal flesh." (Galaxy 5.)

PUER NOBIS NASCITUR. K. K. Davis. "As it fell upon a night." (Galaxy 1291.)

OLD HUNDREDTH. R. Vaughan Williams. The Old Hundredth Psalm Tune, "All people that on earth do dwell." (Oxford.)

VENITE ADOREMUS. Leo Sowerby. "The snow lay on the ground." (Gray 2240.)

CRADLE HYMN. Leo Sowerby. "Hush, my dear." (Gray 2492.)

JOANNA. Eric Thiman. "Immortal, invisible." (Novello 1140.)

ABERYSTWYTH. Parry-Coleman. "Jesus, Lover of my soul." (Oxford E45.)

OLD 124TH. Gustav Holst. "Turn back, O man." (Galaxy 6.)

RATISBON. Healey Willan. "Christ whose glory fills the skies." (Concordia HA2006.)

ST. COLUMBA. Edward Bairstow. "The King of Love my Shepherd is." (Oxford A46.)

Part Six

EDUCATING THE CONGREGATION TO SING HYMNS

CHAPTER **11** *Factors Influencing Congregational Singing*

What makes a particular congregation sing the kind of hymns it does in the way it does? Why does one congregation in a city have superior congregational singing while another church of the same denomination in that locality seems to be made up largely of nonsingers?

There are many influences, some remote, others very direct, which play upon the singing of every congregation. Leaders interested in improvement of singing should understand them if they desire to act wisely and efficiently.

National influences. It can truthfully be said that our church people generally want to sing. Through the secular media of public school music instruction, recorded music, radio and TV, and local concert series, a musically skilled and literate nation is emerging. In the ecclesiastical field, top-flight choir colleges of sacred music have sent thousands of graduates to all corners of the land to build congregational and choral music and to teach in colleges and seminaries. Agencies like the American Guild of Organists, the Hymn Society of America, and the Department of Worship and the Arts of the National Council of the Churches of Christ bring together leaders in church music and worship to share ideas and to develop practical programs. National revival campaigns such as Billy Graham's have pronounced effects upon the music in many churches.

Denominational influences. Each denomination has its particular tradition of hymn singing. Lutherans and Episcopalians, for example, with their liturgical worship have generally maintained high standards of hymnody.

The authorized hymnals of each denomination play a large part in molding the tastes of the congregation. Of equal or greater importance, in the writer's opinion, are the church school hymnals, because permanent attitudes toward hymns are established during the early, formative years.

Some denominations have top-level departments of music for the development of church-wide music programs. Others depend mainly upon the guidance of regular staffs of the official Christian education boards. Our church radio programs, music classes in leadership schools, articles in the church press, music leadership in denominational conventions and conferences, summer schools of church music, music instruction in our seminaries and schools of Christian education—each of these agencies contributes to denominational understanding of music and its potentialities in the church.

Community influences. The cultural level of a community will be reflected quite definitely in the singing of a congregation. Therefore a wealthy suburban church next to a college campus will probably have a type of singing considerably different from a mission church in a mountain cove or mill town. Incidentally, one is not necessarily more effective spiritually than the other. The excellence of the local public school music program will make itself felt in the churches. A steady diet of hillbilly singing broadcast daily into the local homes will condition the musical tastes of congregations.

Local congregational influences. A spiritually vital congregation will enter much more readily into fervent praise than will a dispirited group. The minister, more than any other person, influences the hymnody of the people. The enthusiasm for hymn singing in the pews is very apt to be a reflection of the enthusiasm in the pulpit. A congregation which can engage a full-time minister of music to train a series of choirs has taken a definite step toward a singing church. A capable organist or pianist who skillfully plays the hymns Sunday after Sunday can almost compel a people to sing. The hymnological tastes of the Sunday school superintendent and department heads are inevitably absorbed by the children and young people. We should not forget the vociferous enthusiasm for certain kinds of music found in some adult Bible classes. Also very important in many congregations is the cross-fertilization of musical tastes caused by the large proportion of members reared in other denominations.

A pipe organ with clear ensemble, easy to hear but not overpowering, is a vital factor in promoting better singing. Likewise important, but less frequently realized, is the effect of faulty acoustical treatment of the walls and ceiling of the church. Far too many sanctuaries, overtreated with absorbent acoustical blocks, carpets, draperies, and cushions, are insufficiently reflective. Congregational singers, unable to hear themselves easily, actually experience a certain amount of frustration.

Some of these influences, barely catalogued above, are beyond the control of local leadership. Other factors can definitely be regulated. Some have already been discussed in previous chapters. Others will now be presented. First, we will consider the layman's private study and contemplation of hymn texts. Next, we will deal with the family's influence on an individual's attitude toward hymnody. Then, in widening circles, we will discuss the individual Christian as he receives the impress of church school music, the music of the formal Sunday worship, and, beyond the local situation, the hymn singing of church conferences and conventions.

12 The Private Devotional Use of Hymns

The central spring of hymnody is in the heart of the individual Christian as he is moved by the Holy Spirit. Each person must ponder and absorb in private the meaning of the hymns before great congregational singing can be achieved. Dr. Louis Benson wrote: "It is only the precedent appropriation of the hymn's message by each individual heart that makes its congregational singing worthwhile."[1] Much of the meaning of a hymn will remain unfathomed if we depend on congregational singing alone to reveal the message. During ordinary singing, the syllables and words pass before the consciousness at a speed of a second or less per word. We cannot fully grasp the relationship and sequence of ideas at this speed.

Therefore a Christian should seize the many opportunities which are afforded for reading and contemplating hymn texts. Some of our greatest hymns, after all, were written for private use (for example, the hymns of Bishop Ken). The hymnal is a rich source of devotional literature and can well be used in the home as a prayer book to accompany the Bible in daily devotions. Some would like to read through the hymnal consecutively. Others might prefer to choose hymns which fit their needs of the moment. The Topical Index is a help in this instance.

The standard church hymnal is usually employed for this daily reading. However, there are specialized collections of hymns planned specifically for private reading rather than for congregational singing. Erik Routley's *Hymns and the Faith* has the texts of forty-nine hymns with several pages of interpretation accompanying each. See also H. U. Sims' 150 *Great Hymns in the English Language* (Dietz Press).

An interesting example of a denominational program to encourage hymn reading is the publication by the Moravians of the little volume of *Daily Texts*. Each year hundreds of thousands of these pocket-sized books, printed in more than a score of different languages, are sent to Christians of many denominations and lands. Suggested Bible readings are listed for each day of the year. In addition there is printed a brief text from Scripture *and a few lines from a hymn*. This custom of distributing "Watchwords" and hymn texts began at Herrnhut in Germany about 1725, under the direction of Count Zinzendorf. The addition of these hymn texts, in the words of the Preface, "would lead to a right understanding of the texts and suggest the application of the truths to the individual heart."[2]

Many members of the congregation spend a fruitful few minutes during the Sunday morning prelude reading the texts of the three hymns listed in the bulletin or on the hymn boards. Then when the hymn is announced and is being played over, they again glance over the words to prepare themselves for thoughtful, attentive singing.

Those Christians who have leisurely pondered the truths of great hymns will find William Cowper's words true:

> Sometimes a light surprises
> > The Christian while he sings;
> It is the Lord, who rises
> > With healing in His wings.[3]

CHAPTER **13** *Hymns in the Family Circle*

In 1557, twenty-one years after John Calvin settled in Geneva, a visitor to that city recorded the following account in his diary:

> "A most interesting sight is offered in the city on the weekdays, when the hour for the sermon approaches. As soon as the first sound of the bell is heard, all shops are closed, all conversation ceases, all business is broken off, and from all sides the people hasten to the nearest meeting-house. There each one draws from his pocket a small book which contains the psalms with notes, and out of full hearts, in the native speech, the congregation sings before and after the sermon. Every one testifies to me how great consolation and edification is derived from this custom."[1]

In those days the hymnal accompanied the Christians into their homes and daily lives. Nowadays the hymnal is usually part of the church furniture "not to be removed from the pews." At one time the Bible, chained to the pulpit, was heard by the people only at divine service on the Sabbath. Now a copy of the Holy Scriptures is in most Christian homes and, through pocket editions, it accompanies Christians in the daily walks and crises of life.

The hymnal then must be restored to the Christian homes of our lands. One writer has described Luther's dealings with the hymn in these words: "He took it out of liturgies and put it into people's hearts and homes, that when they had learned it and loved it, they might bring it to the church and sing it together."

Here are some suggestions for concerned leaders.

1. The church office could stock a supply of hymnals to be sold to members. A note in the bulletin and a word from the pulpit could stress the importance of private ownership of hymnals and could urge the purchase of copies from the church office.

2. The bulletin could carry a list of suggested uses of hymns in the home.

3. Any impetus toward music appreciation given the children by the family will be reflected in improved congregational singing. Membership in a children's choir, the gift of a record collection, and private music instruction are a few examples of activities which in maturity should produce a musically literate and eager layman.[2]

4. Parents should request piano teachers to include hymn playing in the private music tuition of their children. The church needs an ample supply of capable pianists. The pianos in the church building might be made available for practice.

5. Many families frequently sing a hymn stanza as a blessing at mealtime. "For the beauty of the earth," "Now thank we all our God," "Fairest Lord Jesus," or the Doxology are suggestions. Some hymnals even include a few graces written specifically for use at mealtime.[3]

6. Many mothers and fathers tuck their children into bed with a prayer and a quiet evening hymn. These hymns will ever afterward be associated with the tender trustfulness of early childhood.

7. Families can enjoy informal singing of hymns as a family group or in company with invited friends. Some ministers set an example by inviting the young people of the church to their home for a song fest. *Rejoice and Sing* is an excellent collection of about 80 hymns and 80 folk songs and rounds. Vest-pocket size, it is admirably suited for informal use.[4]

Lee Hastings and Harold Friedell prepared a fine book just for this purpose called *Hymns for Children and Grownups* (Farrar, Straus, and Young).

At Christmas time for a number of years, our family has joined with several other family groups in singing carols. It is one of the high spots of that season. Here are three good collections: A *Little Carol Book* (Cooperative Recreation Service), *Christmas Carols and Choruses* (Hall & McCreary), and *Noels* edited by Obern-dorfer (Fitz-Simmons).

We are all familiar with Robert Burns' classic description of the Scottish father in "The Cotter's Saturday Night" who gathers his family to hear the Scripture and to sing the metrical psalms:

> They chant their artless notes in simple guise,
> They tune their hearts, by far the noblest aim;
> Perhaps *Dundee's* wild-warbling measures rise,
> Or plaintive *Martyrs*, worthy of the name;
> Or noble *Elgin* beets the heaven-ward flame,
> The sweetest far of Scotia's holy lays:
>
> . . . .
>
> From scenes like these, old Scotia's grandeur springs,
> That makes her lov'd at home, rever'd abroad.[5]

8. Hymnals make excellent gifts. Some churches which follow the Hymn-of-the-Month plan give a hymnal to each person who memorizes all of the hymns listed for that year.

Dr. Benson sums up the matter in this manner:

> So inspiring and uplifting can the spiritual ministry of poetry and music to human lives be made that I venture to propose this task and opportunity of getting the hymnal back into the homes and hands and hearts of Christian people as one of the most rewarding that can engage us.[6]

CHAPTER 14 *Church School Hymnody*

The quality of hymn singing in the formal Sunday morning worship is determined largely by the hymnody produced in the church school. For obvious reasons the musical tastes and skills of a congregation are largely established during the formative years in the educational system of the congregation. A less formal atmosphere, smaller groups, a teaching environment, intimate contact with interested teachers, impressionable early years—these factors make it important that training in hymn singing be of high quality in the church school.

Action toward improvement usually begins with a concern in the heart of some individual connected with the church school, frequently the director of Christian education. It would be quite appropriate for this individual to suggest and urge that "Church School Hymnody" be the subject of earnest, wise consideration by the Christian education committee, teachers' council, church staff, or some other responsible planning group. In one or more meetings this group could establish policies and map out a program which would ennoble the lives of all members of the church school and would lift the spirit of the congregational singing.

Gradual Approach

Any progress in lifting the tastes and desires of a group of church students will come slowly and it should be accompanied by kind consideration for the background and needs of all groups of students. Specifically I have in mind members of adult Bible classes who have been taught by church leaders in former years to love certain types of hymns. These hymns constitute their worship music and they have a right to the satisfaction received in singing them. However, they can also be taught to love many other hymns if a wise, gradual educational plan is followed.

Single Standard

It is well-nigh fatal to hold one standard in the more formal church worship services and then "let the bars down" in Sunday school. Certain denominations use in the formal church service an authorized hymnal containing a wide selection of good hymns, and then in the Sunday school they employ a paper-backed song book which has little relation to the authorized hymnal. It is very unwise to train children in one type of Sunday school hymnody and then to expect them to enjoy and appreciate church hymnody. We will be training a generation of Christians who will always find worship somewhat frustrating. Their plaint will be that of their fathers, "Why can't we sing something we know?"

Good Hymnals

Several denominations (such as the Episcopal) generally use the authorized church hymnal in the Sunday school. This plan has much to commend it. The writer is in favor of this custom down to about the third grade. Other denominational groups have provided a series of graded hymnals, adapted to the needs of the various age levels.

The United Presbyterian Church U.S.A. (Westminster Press, Philadelphia) has published graded hymnals of considerable merit.

The best children's hymnal which has come to my attention is *The Canyon Hymnal for Boys and Girls* (Canyon Press). It has 109 hymns for children from the first to the sixth grade. Three editions are published:

1. The Leader's Edition includes all 109 hymns complete with three-part harmonies. The chords are the same as in standard hymnals and no intervals are beyond an octave in a hand-span. Accompanying each hymn is pertinent information to aid in introducing the

hymn. Definitions of unfamiliar words (underlined in the score) are included. Then there are helpful "Do's" and "Dont's" for leaders of Sunday school singing.
2. The Junior Edition is a melody-only edition including all 109 hymns arranged serially from the first through the sixth grade.
3. The Primary Edition includes 40 hymns—identical with the first three grades of the Junior Edition.

A majority of the hymns are found in the better standard hymnals. For example, all but four of the tunes are in *The Hymn-book* (Presbyterian 1955).

Another excellent children's hymnal, produced by Lutherans, is *Our Songs of Praise*, edited by E. W. Klammer (Concordia). Available in a melody children's edition and a full music accompanist's edition, it contains 147 hymns and songs of high quality.

One of the most versatile youth hymnals is *The Youth Hymnary*, edited by Lester Hostetler (Faith & Life Press, Newton, Kansas). It has many fine features which will commend themselves to young people, such as canons, descants, spirituals, part songs, in addition to hymns.

Student Needs

Adult teachers and superintendents are likely to continue teaching the songs and tunes which they themselves were taught as children. In some cases this practice will only perpetuate a provincial, lopsided type of hymnody. These leaders should conscientiously evaluate current trends in hymn singing and, when possible, give the students the best hymns of the entire Christian church.

Types of Hymns

What hymns should be sung? The church school planning group should make sure that its students learn a central nucleus of great hymns. Such a planning group is similar in many ways to the curriculum committee of a public school system. These public educators do not leave to chance the introduction of the poetry of Shakespeare and Wordsworth. They decide whose poetry shall be introduced in which grade of school.

The hymns actually used in the church school are determined

in part by the tastes of the department superintendents, the pianistic abilities of the players, the caliber of the hymnals, and the suggestions of the lesson material. However, the Christian education committee should try to control to a large extent the type of hymns sung in church school.

It would appear that problems of high standards in Sunday school hymnody are not peculiar to North America. John Mercer Hunter was minister of Abbottshall Church, Kirkcaldy, when the *Manual of Church Praise* According to the Use of the Church of Scotland was issued in 1932. He wrote the stimulating chapter on "Praise in the Sunday School and Children's Services." Speaking of the use of inferior songs in these exercises, he writes:

> It appears that those who are responsible for these selections are mainly earnest laymen who are enthusiastically concerned with what are called "bright" services. By "hearty" singing, an impression of being successful is readily given and conveyed—that, indeed, some real religious work is being accomplished by "one long shout." It would appear that they do not consider such questions as: Will these little children, who are entrusted to our care for their spiritual nourishment, recall these hymns with pride in their later years? Will they turn to them in hours of adult difficulty and danger? Will they make parodies of them at football matches? Will they get from them a worthy conception of religion? Do they foster reverence, or create the spirit of worship? Will they ever be asked to sing them in church? . . . if the children appear to prefer the poor material it is not because they really prefer it, but because they have had no opportunity of learning what is good.[1]

Graded Hymns

Not only should the committee ensure, so far as is possible, the use of valuable hymns, but this group should also make up its mind about graded hymns. Without a doubt, some hymns like "I think when I read that sweet story of old" are meant for children. The location of "Now in the days of youth" in the graded series is apparent. Then there are many hymns which can be grasped only by the mature mind.

Because of obvious levels of hymns and human understanding,

many leaders have insisted on giving children only children's hymns. It is my firm opinion that certain great hymns of the church can be introduced gradually from the child's earliest years in the church school. When the Junior Department is reached, the number can be increased. The teachers who maintain that we must give the child only those hymns that he can fully understand, do not hesitate to teach the Lord's Prayer and the 23rd Psalm, neither of which is fully understood by the most mature saint. Speaking to this point, John Hunter wrote, "It is not necessary to know all there is to be known about a picture, a poem, or a play, before we can appreciate it or derive benefit from it."[2]

To assist a local planning group to have some idea of hymns to be taught in the various departments of the Sunday school, the following graded list is appended. It is suggested that during the several years a student is in a particular department, the hymns for that age level be taught. Naturally a number of other hymns, desired by teachers and lesson planners, will also be taught during this period. And, of course, some leaders will want to shift hymns from one age level to another and perhaps speed up the learning process. However, the use of such a master list will assure an acquaintance with many great hymns by the time the child has grown up. The letters P and E preceding the numbers refer to *The Hymnbook* (Presbyterian 1955) and *The Hymnal 1940* (Episcopal) respectively.

Primary: Grades 1-3. Ages 6-8 years.

> Away in a manger, P157, E43.
> Doxology, P544, E139.
> Fairest Lord Jesus, P135, E346.
> Father, we thank Thee for the night, P467, E240.
> It fell upon a summer day (First two stanzas), P461.
> O little town of Bethlehem, P171, E21.
> Saviour, teach me, day by day, P457, E428.
> Silent night, P154, E33.
> Tell me the stories of Jesus, P459.
> This is my Father's world, P101.
> When morning gilds the skies, P41, E367.
> With happy voices ringing, P463.

Junior: Grades 4-6. Ages 9-11 years.

All beautiful the march of days, P96.
All things bright and beautiful, P456, E311.
Come, Thou Almighty King, P244, E271.
Come, ye thankful people, come, P525, E137.
Day is dying in the west, P65.
Father, lead me day by day, P458.
For the beauty of the earth, P2, E296.
God who made the earth, P466, E248.
God, who touchest earth with beauty, P102.
Good Christian men, rejoice, P165, E31.
Hark, the herald angels sing, P163, E27.
Holy, Holy, Holy! Lord God Almighty, P11, E266.
Jesus Christ is risen today, P204, E85.
Joy to the world, P161, E319.
Let us with a gladsome mind, P28, E308.
Lord, Thy Word abideth, P252, E399.
Morning has broken, P464.
O beautiful for spacious skies, P510.
Onward, Christian soldiers, P350, E557.
Remember all the people, P495, E262.
We would see Jesus; lo! His star is shining, P183.
We've a story to tell to the nations, P504.

Junior High: Grades 7-9. Ages 12-14 years.

All hail the power of Jesus' name, P132, E355.
Faith of our fathers! living still, P348, E393.
God the Omnipotent, P487, E523.
Heralds of Christ, P498.
In Christ there is no East or West, P479, E263.
Jesus shall reign, P496, E542.
Jesus, Thou Joy of loving hearts, P215, E485.
O day of rest and gladness, P70, E474.
Once in royal David's city, P462, E236.
O Thou whose feet have climbed, P468, E507.
Praise the Lord: ye heavens, adore Him, P3.
The Church's one Foundation, P437, E396.
The King of love my Shepherd is, P106, E345.
Where cross the crowded ways, P507, E498.

Senior High: Grades 10-12. Ages 15-17 years.

All creatures of our God and King, P100, E307.
All my heart this night rejoices, P172, E32.

Be Thou my Vision, P303.
Breathe on me, Breath of God, P235, E375.
Built on the Rock, P432.
Dear Lord and Father of mankind, P416, E435.
Father eternal, Ruler of creation, P486, E532.
Glorious things of thee are spoken, P434, E385,
God is our Refuge and our Strength, P381.
God is working His purpose out, P500, E538.
He who would valiant be, P345, E563.
Hills of the North, rejoice, P478.
How firm a foundation, P369, E564.
I bind my heart this tide, P286.
In the cross of Christ I glory, P195, E336.
Joyful, joyful, we adore Thee, P21, E281.
Lead on, O King Eternal, P332, E554.
Lord Jesus, think on me, P270, E417.
Make me a captive, Lord, P308.
Not alone for mighty empire, P512, E145.
Now in the days of youth, P469.
Now, on land and sea descending, P67.
Now woods and wolds are sleeping, P66, E181.
O brother man, fold to thy heart, P474, E493.
O Morning Star, how fair and bright, P415, E329.
Praise ye the Lord, the Almighty, P1, E279.
Rejoice, ye pure in heart, P407, E579.
Shepherd of eager youth, P471, E362.
Take Thou our minds, dear Lord, P306.
Through the night of doubt and sorrow, P475, E394.
We would be building, P470.
Who trusts in God, a strong abode, P375.

Young Adults: College Age.

A mighty Fortress is our God, P91, E551.
Ah, holy Jesus, how hast Thou offended, P191, E71.
Beneath the cross of Jesus, P190, E341.
Christ of the Upward Way, P295.
Draw Thou my soul, O Christ, P284.
Eternal Father, strong to save, P521, E512.
God be in my head, P395, E466.
Guide me, O Thou great Jehovah, P339, E434.
I to the hills will lift mine eyes, P377.
If thou but suffer God to guide thee, P344.
Immortal Love, forever full, P229, E360.
O God of earth and altar, P511, E521.

O God, our Help in ages past, P111, E289.
O sacred Head, now wounded, P194, E75.
O Son of Man, our Hero strong and tender, P217, E364.
Once to every man and nation, P361, E519.
Rise, my soul, and stretch thy wings, P330.
Soldiers of Christ, arise, P362, E552.
Spirit of God, descend, P236.
The God of Abraham praise, P89, E285.
Thou hidden Source of calm repose, P423.
Turn back, O man, P490, E536.
We are living, we are dwelling, P356.

Practical Suggestions

1. *Use the church musician.* The musician at work in the church is there for the same ultimate purpose as the director of Christian education and the minister. It is their desire to lead others into fuller Christian experience. The musician, working with the leaders of the church school, will always want to use his abilities to further the ideas expressed in the lesson material. By constantly working together with the department heads, the church musician can greatly enrich the weekly programs of worship and study.

2. *A specific church school and choir hymn-learning project.* In an effort to improve the present condition and to ensure the quality of future congregational singing, the Druid Hills Presbyterian Church of Atlanta, Georgia (Mr. and Mrs. Haskell Boyter, Ministers of Music), have engaged in an experiment which is a unique approach to the solution of the problem.

Instead of urging the adults to participate more wholeheartedly in the singing of familiar hymns and in learning new ones, they have attacked the problem from the 7-year-old children up through the youth choirs.

In choir rehearsals, twenty-five new hymns were taught the children during the season (October to June).[3] In addition to this group work, a hymn-memorizing contest was announced from October 15 to May 15. The rules were as follows:

Each child was to

1. Memorize the melody.
2. Memorize the first stanza.

3. Sing melody and first stanza from memory unaccompanied, before the "listening committee."

Adequate records were kept and tabulated by a "Hymn Chairman," with monthly announcements of who was ahead in the contest.

Such remarkable response was received that the "listening committee" had to be doubled within eight weeks' time!

The important feature regarding this project is the fact that these hymns were *selected and taught by the parents of the choristers*—the first wedge in a "family" project! Later, when enthusiasm was rampant, a "Family Hymn-Sing" was announced, with recognition to be given the 100% families who were present. There were 23 families who were 100% present! Between 250 and 300 people attended and sang more enthusiastically than most of the Sunday morning congregations. The Hymn-Sing was held Sunday afternoon between 3:30 and 4:30 o'clock. The fact that this "Sing" was announced as lasting exactly one hour played a large part in its success. All the promotional communications stated that even if the congregation were in the middle of a hymn, they could count on exactly one hour for this project. Besides improving congregational singing, it is hoped that through this "family affair" the old custom of family singing in the homes may be revived, at least to a certain extent.

A second "Sing" was held a month later with almost 400 present, and 27 families were 100% there.

A revealing fact is the *exposure to 19 new hymns* besides many old or familiar hymns which were sung during the two 1-hour sessions. The boys and girls who already knew these new hymns were urged to *hold hymnals with their fathers and mothers,* and thus lead them in the learning of new materials—and at the same time this feeling of "family togetherness" was felt more and more strongly.

There were 972 hymns sung from memory by the 7- to 13-year-olds in the two choirs from October 15 to May 15. This wide experience with one stanza memorized was more valuable, it was felt, than many stanzas of fewer hymns. After all, all the ages represented could read any number of stanzas, once they were acquainted with the hymn tune.

The follow-up of the 1957-58 project was the further extension into the church school, and eventually into the congregational singing, of the hymn study started through the children's choirs. With a nucleus of approximately 400 from the "Family Hymn-Sing," these, in turn, became "torch bearers," so to speak, in the church school in their respective departments.

The minister of music, the director of Christian education, and a council from the departments of the church school chose the hymns to be used in a church-wide Hymn Festival in the early spring of 1959. These were sung throughout the year in the classes and then, when festival time came, the church school *sponsored* it as a part of the Christian education program, and they were *assisted* by the music department! This again increased the impact of the fusion of the two departments—the ultimate goal toward which all church leaders should work.

During the 1958-59 church year, interest increased beyond expectation. Almost 1300 hymns were sung!

The contest was extended to the playing of hymns also—on any instrument chosen. As Mrs. Boyter states: "In this way we hope to *grow our own* Sunday school pianists and instrumentalists in time. Seventy-five per cent of my junior choirs are studying privately, so why not capitalize on this! Some of them are going to make splendid pianists and soloists. The winner in this area of the contest played 108 hymns on clarinet and a large number on piano also."

When five or ten minutes were available in some rehearsals, and opportunity was given for children to choose what they would sing, almost invariably hymns which they had learned during the year were requested.

Besides encouraging the learning of hymn tunes and words, Mrs. Boyter taught the singers to classify hymns by pattern or form. "As we learned hymns, we listed them under their own pattern and in time we will have quite a repertoire of hymns of different patterns. First we did this by colors. For instance, in singing 'Joyful, joyful, we adore Thee,' we had red, yellow, green, and blue strips of construction paper from which to choose.

"After the choir sang the first line of this hymn, we decided to call this theme red. Then the second line was sung and the question asked whether it was the same or different. The choir said, 'Same.' 'O.K., pick up another red strip.

" 'This is the third line. Is it the same or different?' 'Different.' 'O.K., pick up another color.

" 'This is the fourth line. Is it the same or different?'

" 'It is the same as one and two.' 'O.K., what do we have, class?' 'Red, red, yellow, red.'

"The children *loved* this."

During the season, 1959-60, Mrs. Boyter had a piano-playing class in which she taught the children how to play for hymn-singing groups in the Sunday school. Eventually she should have good pianists for all the departments.

3. *Services of worship.* If the department assembles for worship before or after the study period, it is a good idea occasionally to devote all or a part of this time to learning a new hymn. Sometimes it is profitable to instruct the group in basic attitudes toward hymn singing.

A prominent director of Christian education told me about an interesting service with the youth of the church school in which she serves. As part of an assembly devoted to hymn singing, she had asked five boys to tell their fellow students about John Wesley's five Directions for Singing. (See chapter 3.) She reported that each one in his own words did an effective job of communicating the intent of each rule. The singing of that church school was improved by this explanation of Wesley's ideas.

4. *Urge Sunday school teachers to use hymn texts as teaching aids.* If the story of Jacob at Bethel is to be taught, the teacher could have the class open the hymnal to the hymns, "O God of Bethel, by whose hand" and "Nearer, my God, to Thee," both of which have something to say about the meaning of this notable Biblical incident. The doctrine of the Trinity is illumined by such hymns as "Ancient of Days" and "Come, Thou Almighty King."

The Christian attitude toward the Sabbath is set forth in "O day of rest and gladness." Students learn much about the church from "The Church's one Foundation," and about Christian brotherhood from "In Christ there is no East or West."

Teachers can be reminded to refer to the table of contents or the topical index of any superior hymnal to find suggested hymn titles bearing on a specific doctrine or topic.

In this connection we might recall with profit the words of the Rev. Archibald Alexander, first professor of Princeton Theological Seminary, who in a preface to a long-forgotten hymnal which he edited, wrote:

> Evangelical hymns are peculiarly suited to be the vehicle of gospel truth to the young and ignorant. It is a fact that unlettered Christians retain in their minds more of the gospel in the words of the spiritual songs which they are accustomed to sing than in any other form, and children can perhaps be taught the truths of religion in this way, more effectually than in any other . . . the understanding is reached with most certainty through the feelings of the heart.[4]

5. *Add some good books on hymnody to the church school library.* Teachers and students alike should have a few choice reference books to consult in preparing lessons and services built on hymns. Some volumes have been mentioned in the Bibliography.

6. *Organize a hymn-playing class for Sunday school pianists.* Ask the church organist or some capable pianist to spend several hours with the Sunday school pianists. Some of the hymns on the list just given could furnish a basis for study. The leader might outline and illustrate methods of playing hymns, perhaps following some of the procedures suggested in chapter 9. Members of the class might be willing to play hymn tunes planned for their class sessions and to have their playing analyzed by the class.

7. *Adopt an orderly maintenance schedule for church school pianos.* It is a good idea to arrange with a capable tuner to go over the pianos several times a year, perhaps two or three weeks after the winter furnace heat is turned on and again several weeks after it is turned off. Some such scheme would ensure satisfying tones for preludes and congregational accompaniment.

Congregational singing is shaped largely by the training in singing given the children of the church. This is why it is so important to plan wisely for the improvement of the music in the Sunday school.

CHAPTER 15

How a Layman Learns a Hymn

A hymn includes both words and music. Therefore when a churchgoer opens his hymnal on Sunday morning, he sees in front of him two kinds of text—words and music.

Perhaps the minister has announced Frances Wile's hymn of nature "All beautiful the march of days," with its lovely English folk melody FOREST GREEN. I have deliberately selected for illustration a relatively unfamiliar hymn so that many of the readers will probably have to read both texts at sight, unaided by memory.

At the first of this hymn our layman sees this English text:

"All beautiful the march of days,
As seasons come and go."

Accompanying this English text, he sees this musical notation:

Which of these two texts do you understand most readily? Which can you read aloud immediately at sight?

The members of the usual congregation are probably one hundred per cent literate when it comes to reading English text, whereas they may not be twenty-five per cent literate in reading music text. Of course, the ability to read music varies enormously from place to place. There are exceptional congregations such as the student body of a choir college which can read at sight any hymn tune in the book.

The average layman, seeing the opening English text of Miss Wile's hymn, obviously can read it aloud immediately with his fellow worshipers.

> All beautiful the march of days,
>   As seasons come and go;
> The Hand that shaped the rose hath wrought
>   The crystal of the snow;
> Hath sent the hoary frost of heaven,
>   The flowing waters sealed,
> And laid a silent loveliness
>   On hill and wood and field.[1]

He readily understands that the hymn is about the divine order and beauty found in the unfolding procession of days from season to season.

However, when our layman sees the musical notation of this opening phrase, unless he is exceptional, he will be unable to hum or sing the phrase exactly. He may be able to make his voice go up when the second note goes up but he does not know how far to leap. Further, there is the bothersome question of how long to hold each note—a question, incidentally, which rarely crosses the mind of some singers.

In other words, he is asked to sing both words and music and he frequently knows how to read only the words! The average layman thus far simply has not been taught to read musical notation as well as he has been taught to read English.

How, then, did our layman learn the several score hymn tunes in his possession? He learned them by rote. From earliest childhood he heard them sung again and again. All his life he has heard his parents, his Sunday school friends, the church choir, and others sing, for example, "Onward, Christian soldiers." Years ago this melodic structure was deposited deep in his musical consciousness. It is an old, old favorite.

Since the average layman learns a tune by hearing it repeated until he has memorized it, obviously he can grasp a simple tune with short phrases more quickly. No wonder anybody can sing "Three blind mice"! Two short musical themes are repeated, one of them five times, the other three times, to form this popular little ditty.

Sing over to yourself the first stanza of "Wonderful words of life" and observe the repetition of text and musical phrase. The same is true of the chorus of "Tell me the old, old story" and many other gospel songs.

Many hymns are just as singable. Study the repetition of theme in "Silent Night," "Fairest Lord Jesus," and "Finlandia." It is true also that there are factors other than mere thematic repetition which contribute to singability.

My main point at the moment is that, since our layman usually cannot read the music, we must give him plenty of opportunity to hear a new tune if we want him to sing it. If we ever have particular difficulty in teaching a new melody, just recall that millions of Americans have learned "The Star-Spangled Banner." It is not an easy tune to sing.

Most members will sing when an old favorite like "Faith of our fathers" is announced, but many laymen will not even attempt a tune if they have never heard it before. Many of these nonsingers can be changed to enthusiastic, willing singers if the leader will observe the generally accepted laws of learning.

The law of readiness. We learn when we are ready and eager to learn. Many laymen, seeing a new hymn listed in the bulletin and hearing its strange tune played over, are quite unready to sing it. Some interesting fact about the hymn's origin or text or tune will at least focus attention on the hymn. As we have earlier said, certain ministers have their choir sing a new hymn as an anthem on the Sunday before the congregation is asked to sing it. While the choir is singing the hymn, the people are requested to read it. Then the following Sunday the congregation anticipates the hymn and is much more ready to join in the service of praise.

The law of effect. When a learning experience has been pleasant, there will be desire for repetition. Frequently a layman who cannot read music feels frustrated while trying a hymn for the first time. He should realize that even experienced choristers have to try and retry a new anthem or melody.

If the minister is obviously enjoying the singing experience and the choir is outlining a clear, strong melody, if his neighbors in the pew are making an honest attempt, then the layman is quite likely to find the new tune attractive and to discover that his first encounter with it is a pleasant one.

The law of repetition. When a fact or experience is repeated sufficiently often, it becomes a part of memory, or is fixed as a habit. It is futile to try a new hymn, then drop it for six months. Fix it by repeating it occasionally within a period of a month or so. Presently it becomes an old favorite.

Professor Ray Brown of General Theological Seminary (Episcopal), New York, suggests the following three stages for the selection and introduction of new hymns:

> 1. Make a list of all the hymns in the present repertory. Keep all of them, good and bad, in use. Avoid the introduction of anything else without careful selection and preparation.
>
> 2. Make a list of the best hymns, considering both words and music, which are needed in the repertory for all the seasons of the Church Year, and for certain Holy Days and other occasions when hymns are to be sung. Add to this some of the best general hymns, having in mind the appropriateness of some of them for special uses. Then teach a hymn from this list to the congregation from time to time, not more often than once a month.
>
> 3. Drop from the repertory the less desirable hymns by using them less and less frequently and finally not at all; but do this only after several new hymns have been learned and have become popular.
>
> If a congregation is to have such a repertory it must have a chance to sing the numbers in it often enough to keep them in practice. The use of as many as four hymns at each service will make it possible to have most of them recur two or three times a year, which is a practical necessity if the repertory is to be kept up.[2]

Thousands of congregations are led each week into a happy and inspiring exploration of the spiritual treasures of the hymnal. It is a rewarding privilege to introduce a new hymn.

CHAPTER 16 Congregational Rehearsals

A congregational rehearsal might be called a hymn-sing with a definite educational purpose. Hymn practices have been widely used in Britain. The idea is described in detail in *Music and Worship* by Sir Walford Davies and Dr. Harvey Grace. Their chapter on "Congregational Singing" made such good sense to me that I could hardly wait to try out the scheme. This I have done in dozens of different churches. The general response has been that the laymen enthusiastically appreciate practical instruction in hymn singing and receive a new impetus in the service of praise.

After all, our forefathers used to gather for a whole week in a singing school where they not only learned many new hymns but even learned to read notes acceptably. Certainly we ought to be able to devote an hour occasionally to this specific instruction. The minister, the organist, and the choir spend a number of hours each week in preparation for leadership of the Sunday worship. The congregation could also give time to the consideration of its responsibility in the service.

Sir Walford says this about these laymen's rehearsals:

> . . . for congregational singing to become the fine thing it may be, congregational practices are indispensable. Only by such means can the faults that are inevitable in the first singing of an untrained mass be dispelled. Matters of simple discipline are contagious. For example, a congregation without great difficulty may be induced to start a hymn alertly and unanimously by a few minutes of practice and persuasive exhortation devoted to that point.[1]

Another Britisher, Plunket Greene, has given three simple rules for singing which will help a congregation in its hymn singing.[2]

His first suggestion is, "Never stop the *march* of a song." In other words, feel the pulse and keep the hymn moving right to the end.

Second, he says, "Sing mentally through your rests." In congregational singing, this would mean that the people should listen to the playing over of the hymn by the piano or organ and thus get in the singing mood and pace.

Third, "Sing as you speak." That is to say, enunciate the words clearly and concentrate on the text.

Some British churches have these practices a half-hour before the evening service. American congregations might occasionally prefer a brief evening service followed by a hymn practice instead of the usual sermon. A short or long practice at a fellowship supper during the week might find more of the congregation in attendance.

The leader of this practice could be the minister, the choirmaster, or a layman. Anyone with a gift of informal leadership, a singing voice, and a love of hymns could do it. He or she should stand in full view of the people and occasionally might rove up and down the aisles. The conductor's voice is a better teaching medium than playing the tune on the organ. If there is a choir present, it could be asked to sit among the people and occasionally illustrate a snatch of melody. Simple gestures to outline the melody and beat are helpful.[3] Sir Walford Davies suggests that "the less formal and schoolmasterish or ecclesiastical his method, the better."[4] Remember that the people have assembled to sing hymns, not to listen to a lecture on hymnody.

Some new tunes can be taught by playing and singing them over once. Others need a line-by-line method. In teaching a hymn like "I sing the mighty power of God," tune ELLACOMBE (P84), attention is first directed to the text of Isaac Watts which magnificently describes God the Creator and Preserver of all creation. Next, the entire hymn melody could be played over—perhaps without any harmonic support. Then it would help in mastering the entire melody if the congregation were made aware that the second and fourth lines are identical. After singing (or playing) the second line of the melody to the congregation, and perhaps indicating the general contour of the phrase with the dip in the middle, let the people sing the second line of the first stanza. Then to anchor it, repeat this phrase but use the words of the last line. In each singing you might show how the phrase draws to a satisfactory close and gives a feeling of completion.

Now you are ready to sing the first phrase of this four-line tune. As it is sung for the people, point out how the last three notes are the only tones different from the second and fourth lines and show how this change lifts the tune to a note of expectancy where the singers are stimulated to look forward to the next phrase. Now let your congregation sing the first line.

You could point out that three-fourths of the hymn tune has already been learned. Then tackle the remaining brace, that is, the third line. Play this third line over, then explain that it is composed of two almost identical phrases, each occupying about half the line. Show that the first seven notes of each half of the line are identical. If you think they would be interested you might even point out how each half of this third line begins with the tonic chord of B flat and ends on the dominant chord of F. Thus the third line ends harmonically in a manner that gives a feeling of nostalgia for the home key of B flat. Now let the people sing this third line, two or three times, perhaps with the three stanzas consecutively.

Now we are ready for the synthesis. Have the congregation now sing the melody straight through with the piano or organ playing only the melody in unison or octaves.

Then, to clinch the hymn by repetition, sing also the second and third stanzas.

By such teaching means, a new text and tune can be readily taught to a group in the church.

It is not inconceivable that present-day congregations might welcome some specific instruction in reading music at occasional laymen's rehearsals. A few minutes devoted to explanation of such symbols as staffs, clefs, measures, time signatures, and note values would yield valuable fruit. Help in planning such instruction can be secured from Howard Shanet's *Learn to Read Music* (Simon and Schuster, 1956).

The rehearsal leader might distribute and explain John Wesley's Rules for Singing. He should also make use of interesting information about the background of hymns, encourage the group to stand in time to sing during the regular service of worship, and generally cultivate the spirit of joyous song. As Luther said, "When we sing, both heart and mind should be cheerful and merry."

It is a good idea to begin and end the congregational hymn practice with familiar hymns. The rehearsal can be varied by singing certain tunes in unison. Other stanzas might be sung in full harmony or antiphonally.

An informal pantomime or simple dramatization of a hymn story would add interest. Some years ago in teaching a congregation the hymn "Be still, my soul" to the tune FINLANDIA, I played a recording of the chorale section of Sibelius' orchestral tone poem "Finlandia."

The leader might even mimeograph and distribute a hymn quiz such as the following one devised by Dr. Kenneth Foreman of Louisville Presbyterian Theological Seminary.[5] Only a portion of the original published quiz is included.

Dr. Foreman says:

> Any number of quizzes could be devised to see whether you (or your class, or your family, or your congregation) understand and are familiar with the words, tunes, and meanings of the hymns you sing. The following is a Bible-hymn quiz. Many of our hymns have Biblical allusions, some very obvious, others less so. See if you can identify those below.
>
> 1. "Holy, Holy, Holy! Lord God Almighty." What "glassy sea" is meant in the second stanza?
> 2. "Joyful, joyful, we adore Thee." What New Testament authority is back of the affirmation "All who live in love are Thine"?
> 3. "Come, Thou Fount of every blessing." What battle monument is referred to in the line, "Here I raise my Ebenezer"?

4. "Come, Thou Almighty King." Where in the Bible is Christ pictured with a sword?

5. "O day of rest and gladness." This is a richly allusive hymn. See how many Bible references you can find. There is one error, no doubt a poetic license, in the lines "Today on weary nations the heavenly manna falls" (found in some hymnbooks). Strictly speaking, this is an incorrect reference. Why?

6. "O God of Bethel, by whose hand." Why the God of "Bethel" instead of Shechem or Zion or some other two-syllable town?

7. "I know not how that Bethlehem's Babe." What Joseph is meant in stanza 3?

8. "Be known to us in breaking bread." To what incident in Christ's life does line 1 refer?

9. "Love divine, all loves excelling." What does "Alpha and Omega be" mean, and where in the Bible is the source of the idea?

10. "O Jesus, Thou art standing." What New Testament passage suggested this hymn?

CHAPTER 17 Hymn Services and Festivals

Some congregations upon occasion spend an entire service singing hymns. Usually the hymns are centered upon a theme and are interspersed with appropriate prayers, Scripture readings, and connective comments. Frequently a choir, quartet, or soloist is present to lead the singing.

Such services may be brief ten-minute parts of a fellowship supper or a half-hour inspirational service of the women's or young people's group or an hour service of worship on Sunday. Incidentally, some congregations have a series of these musical services, perhaps on the first Sunday evening of each month or for the four Sunday evenings of a particular month.

In planning such services, it is probably wise to begin and end with a familiar hymn. In fact, the majority of the hymns perhaps ought to be at least moderately familiar so that the congregation will have a sense of satisfaction. Each detail of the service should be meticulously planned. Vigorous hymns should be alternated with quieter ones for a change of mood. The singing could sometimes be varied by using several descants, faux-bourdons, and varied accompaniments. The definition and reason for these musical devices could be explained. Stories of several of the hymns might be in order. All comments, however, should be brief, clear, and interesting. Omit certain stanzas or have the congregation read occasional ones to rest their voices.

Let the choir or quartet sing some of the stanzas or hymns. In one musical service recently the choir came out of the chancel and scattered among the congregation. The presence of these experienced singers in their midst gave new courage and enthusiasm to the laymen.

We will give first an outline of a service of worship commemorating the life and work of Isaac Watts, the Father of English Hymnody. This order was prepared for the Hymn Society of America by the Rev. Philip S. Watters. It is suggestive only, with the expectation that it could be modified to meet local situations.

PRELUDE

CALL TO WORSHIP *(Solo or Chorus)*
>   Come, let us join our cheerful songs
>   With angels round the throne;
>   Ten thousand thousand are their tongues
>   But all their joys are one.

Tune: NATIVITY   ISAAC WATTS, 1707

HYMN OF PRAISE *From Psalm 117 (Congregation standing)*
>   "From all that dwell below the skies"
Tune: OLD HUNDREDTH   ISAAC WATTS, 1719

RESPONSIVE CALL TO PRAYER *(Congregation standing)*
>   *Minister:* O come, let us worship and bow down: let us kneel before the Lord, our Maker.
>   *People:*   For He is the Lord, our God: and we are the people of His pasture, and the sheep of His hand.
>   *Minister:* Let us pray.

INVOCATION *(In unison. Congregation seated.)*
>   Almighty God, unto whom all hearts are open, all desires known, and from whom no secrets are hid; cleanse the thoughts of our hearts by the inspiration of Thy Holy Spirit, that we may perfectly love Thee, and worthily magnify Thy holy Name, through Jesus Christ our Lord. *Amen.*

THE LORD'S PRAYER

HYMN OF OLD TESTAMENT PROPHECY *Based on Psalm 72*
>   "Jesus shall reign where'er the sun"
Tune: DUKE STREET   ISAAC WATTS, 1719

SCRIPTURE READING *Psalm 98:4, 7-9*

HYMN OF NEW TESTAMENT FULFILLMENT
Based on Psalm 98
"Joy to the world! the Lord is come"
Tune: ANTIOCH   ISAAC WATTS, 1719

PASTORAL PRAYER

CHOIR RESPONSE
To God the only wise,
Our Saviour and our King,
Let all the saints below the skies
Their humble praises bring. *Amen.*
Tune: ST. MICHAEL   ISAAC WATTS, 1707

OFFERING

OFFERTORY *(The Choir)*
"When I survey the wondrous cross"
Tune: HAMBURG   ISAAC WATTS, 1707

CONSECRATION OF OFFERING

HYMN OF JOYOUS FAITH
"Come, we that love the Lord"
Tune: ST. THOMAS   ISAAC WATTS, 1707

SERMON OR ADDRESS

PRAYER

HYMN OF TRUST *From Psalm 90*
"Our God, our Help in ages past"
Tune: ST. ANNE   ISAAC WATTS, 1719

PRAYER *(The Minister. Congregation seated.)*
O God our Father, grant that Thy praises may evermore be en-
riched and made glorious by the beauty and blessing of holy hymns
born of Thy Spirit. May we ever sing with gladness in our hearts,
and show forth Thy praise in worthy and triumphant songs. Let
Thy Spirit so dwell in the hearts of Thy people here and everywhere
that they may be led to sing with grace and deep gratitude as unto
Thee. Grant that all who here find joy in worshiping Thee may be
numbered at last with those who shall sing the new song before the
heavenly throne; through Jesus Christ our Lord who liveth and
reigneth with Thee, O Father, and the Holy Spirit, ever one God,
world without end. *Amen.*

BENEDICTION

POSTLUDE[1]

We do not have space to give detailed plans for each topic which we shall now suggest. They can be planned by anyone who is imaginatively interested in hymnody. The topical, authors', and composers' indexes will be of real help in discovering appropriate hymns. Various handbooks suggested in the Bibliography will give background information for comments and addresses.

Here are some topics with a few hints for their development:

Hymns based on Psalm 23. "The Lord's my Shepherd, I'll not want"; "The King of love my Shepherd is"; "Saviour, like a Shepherd lead us"; "In heavenly love abiding"; and "He leadeth me: O blessed thought" are based in varying degree on the Shepherd Psalm.

God in nature. St. Francis' "All creatures of our God and King"; "Fairest Lord Jesus"; "This is my Father's world"; and "The spacious firmament on high" are but a few of dozens of hymns dealing with the natural world. Projected slide pictures of beautiful natural scenes are sometimes used to emphasize concepts in the hymn stanzas.

History of the Christian Church in hymns. Seven or eight of the significant eras of Christianity could be sketched and emphasized by appropriate hymns. The basic list of hymns in chapter 5 is arranged chronologically and would be a help in selecting hymns of historical importance.

Hymn tunes of great composers. J. S. Bach, PASSION CHORALE and JESU, MEINE FREUDE; Beethoven, HYMN TO JOY; Haydn, AUSTRIAN HYMN; Vaughan Williams, SINE NOMINE—these are but a few examples of tunes written by notable composers. Other appropriate music by these composers might be played in recorded form or by actual performers.

Hymns for family use. A Charlotte, North Carolina church had a service of music to show that hymns do not become a part of a person until he sings them spontaneously at work or at play and at worship. Its purpose was to show how hymns may be used in the home and to stimulate families to form the habit of singing hymns at home. The service consisted of a series of pantomimed pictures portrayed on a stage by members of the congregation while illustrative hymns were sung by special singers or the congregation.

Here were the topics used: Singing at breakfast; Washing dishes; Twins at play; The seamstress (illustrated by the oldest member of congregation); Paper boys whistling; Helping on the farm; The family gathered round the piano; Mother rocking her babe.

Hymn tune preludes. Congregations will enjoy hearing a variety of well-played compositions based on familiar and unfamiliar hymn melodies. Singing of these tunes could be interspersed with the playing or even be combined. See chapter 9 for suggested collections of hymn preludes.

Hymns by famous authors or composers. We have just seen a service devoted to the hymns of Isaac Watts. From time to time the Hymn Society of America issues services printed in inexpensive leaflet form which are based on the life and hymns of a famous author. It has also provided accompanying informative brochures for these services. In addition to Watts, the Society within the past few years has commemorated the hymns of Henry Francis Lyte, Louis F. Benson, John Greenleaf Whittier, Charles Wesley, and Maltbie D. Babcock. Several years ago it sponsored nationwide services commemorating the musical legacy left by Lowell Mason for our hymnals. A minister or church musician could use the patterns of the services mentioned above or could originate his own, including a sketch of the author's life and explanations of the individual hymns.[2]

Women hymn writers. A church women's group might enjoy a service featuring hymns by such writers as Charlotte Elliott, Frances Ridley Havergal, Frances Wile, Katharine Lee Bates, and others.

The Life of Christ in song. It is possible to illustrate much of Christ's life through hymns and appropriate Scripture. The Reverend George L. Knight prepared such a service using Benson's "O sing a song of Bethlehem" as the theme hymn. Its four stanzas deal with Bethlehem, Nazareth, Galilee, and Calvary and Easter.

Bible passages give the background for the particular period in Jesus' life; next, a stanza of the theme hymn is sung; and then several other hymns relating to the life of Christ in that specific period are sung. Many hymnals have a large section of hymns dealing specifically with "Jesus Christ" listed in the table of contents.

Men and women of letters in the hymnal. Whittier, Tennyson, Milton, Addison, Bryant, Bunyan, Chesterton, and Struther are some examples of outstanding literary figures who have contributed hymns.

Hymn writers of various denominations. Many separate branches are represented in the hymnal. Among them are Presbyterian—Bonar and Matheson; Episcopal—Brooks and Heber; Methodist—the Wesleys and North; Baptist—Fawcett; Lutheran—Luther; Quaker—Whittier. A brief sketch of the distinctive contributions of each denomination plus a strong statement of common faith in our Lord should lead to increased interdenominational understanding.

Hymns or tunes of a particular period. The Hymn Society has also sponsored hundreds of services across the country on such topics as "American Hymnody of the 20th century," "The 300th Anniversary of the Scottish Psalter," "The 400th Anniversary of the Genevan Psalter of 1551." Inexpensive pamphlet collections of representative hymns and tunes were issued for such celebrations. Most good hymnals have enough material for such services.

Types of hymn tunes. Hymn tunes are generally classified into types according to style of composition or historical era or national origin. Explanation of these types may be found in some detail in texts listed in the Bibliography. Here are several examples of some of the major types of tunes:

Plainsong: VENI CREATOR, DIVINUM MYSTERIUM
German Chorale: PASSION CHORALE, LOBE DEN HERREN
Genevan Psalm Tune: OLD HUNDREDTH, TOULON
Scottish Psalm Tune: DUNDEE, DUNFERMLINE
18th-Century British: DUKE STREET, MILES' LANE
Victorian Hymn Tune: NICAEA, LANCASHIRE
Contemporary British: SINE NOMINE, CHARTERHOUSE

19th-Century American: OLIVET, MISSIONARY HYMN
Contemporary American: ST. DUNSTAN'S, ST. JOAN
National Folk Melodies: America—PROTECTION (FOUNDA-
TION); England—GREENSLEEVES; Wales—JOANNA; France
—PICARDY; Germany—IN DULCI JUBILO; Holland—
KREMSER; Ireland—SLANE.

The Choristers' Guild of Lynchburg, Virginia presented its combined youth choirs in a Gymanfa Ganu (Welsh singing festival)
which featured such tunes as HYFRYDOL, ABERYSTWYTH,
MEIRIONYDD, LLANFAIR, CWM RHONDDA, AR HYD Y NOS, LLAN-
HERNE, and EBENEZER (TON-Y-BOTEL).

Some of the following titles may suggest a fruitful topic for the
development of a hymn service: Great Doctrines in Hymns;
Metrical Psalms; Hymns by Jews, Protestants, and Roman Cath-
olics; World Fellowship through Hymns; Hymn Writers of Various Professions; Dramatized Hymn Stories; Anonymous Hymn
Writers; Alternate Tunes to Well-Known Hymns; Hymns by Chinese Christians; Hymns of Faith, Hope, and Love; Hymns of the
Inner and Outer Life; Tune Names; The Book of Revelation in
Hymns.

HYMN FESTIVALS

A hymn festival is a celebration of the Christian faith through
congregational song. Each year thousands of Christians in scores
of communities throughout the country join in hymn festivals.
Detroit, Atlanta, Portland, Richmond, New York, and Raleigh are
but a few of the larger cities where hymn festivals have been
organized. These inspiring services, whether denominational or
interdenominational, have been sponsored by such groups as a
rural or urban ministerial association, an organists' guild, a music
club, a church youth committee, a council of churches, or the
Hymn Society of America.

Under expert leadership and surrounded by throngs of singing
Christians, a layman usually gains a completely new experience of
praise through song. He takes back to his congregation a new concept of stimulating, intelligent singing. The seeds of positive
influence planted by such festivals are numberless.

As a specific example let me cite briefly what was done along this line in Richmond, Virginia. The local chapter of the American Guild of Organists, assisted by the Ministerial Association, sponsored a hymn festival for Protestant congregations. Because of the great interest manifested, it was decided to engage the largest civic auditorium available (4,500 capacity). Forty-seven vested choirs with more than a thousand singers were placed in groups of sixty here and there in the vast congregation. Clergymen from Presbyterian, Methodist, Baptist, and Episcopal churches assisted in the actual leadership of the festival.

If this festival had been held in a large church, it probably would have been possible to use the regular hymnal of that church. However, for this large gathering the festival committee printed a sixteen-page booklet, which included not only the order of service but the text and music of the hymns plus Wesley's "Directions for Singing."

The topics for festival services could be drawn from the list of themes given earlier in this chapter. Committees interested in planning a festival are directed to two papers of the Hymn Society of America:

1. Paper V: *Hymn Festival Programs*.
2. Paper XVI: *The Hymn Festival Movement in America*.

CHAPTER **18** *Acoustics and Its Effect on Congregational Singing*

The magnificent tone of a Stradivarius violin depends in large part upon cavity resonance. This means that the vibrations, which leave the strings as the bow presses them, pass into the marvelously shaped interior of the violin. Here the sound waves are selectively modified and amplified so that the tones which emerge and reach the ears of the audience are considered beautiful. A Stradivarius stuffed with cotton would trap these vibrations and seriously and adversely affect the tone of the instrument.

In like manner the cavity of an auditorium, surrounded by the floor, walls, and ceiling, acts upon a tone generated within its confines. The tone of voices, a piano, or organ will either be stultified or will be glorified by the acoustical environment. Consequently it is of enormous importance to a congregation to see that optimum acoustical conditions prevail in the church sanctuary.

A certain generous lady, for example, might like to donate a lovely deep red carpet for the entire church floor. This act of philanthropy might take the keen edge off congregational singing for the duration of the life of the rug. A hard, reflective, waxed cork or rubber tile flooring could conceivably make as splendid a gift and yet retain acoustical vibrancy for the interior.

Sir James Jeans, celebrated British physicist, speaking of this acoustical phenomenon, says in his *Science and Music* that sufficient reverberation in an auditorium

> . . . naturally induces an exhilarating feeling of effortless
> power, not to mention a welcome slurring over of rough-
> nesses and inequalities of force and tempo.

Of a non-reverberant room, he further says that this

> . . . produces the despair of ineffectual struggle: the music
> has only had time to show its blemishes in all their naked-
> ness, and is already dead.[1]

In certain cases, an enthusiastic purveyor of acoustical blocks
might convince an elder who is hard of hearing that he could
catch the parson's words if the ceiling of the church were treated
with his particular brand of acoustical surface. Overlooked are
such possibilities as hearing aids attached to pews or to the elder,
clearer enunciation and more volume from the preacher, or some
form of electronic amplification within the church.

What specifically happens when vibrations leave the throats of
the congregation and minister or the organ pipes? These sound
waves pass through the air until they hit a surface. Here they are
either reflected to some other surface or they are absorbed. Everyone has seen the little holes in acoustical blocks. The vibrations
pass into these holes and are trapped. Most of the sound does not
get out again.

In public dining rooms, in halls of school buildings, and in all
places where much noise is generated and little sound is wanted
—these are places where sound control and dampening are indicated.

But the interior of a church is an instrument—an instrument of
God—and it should be so formed that His praise, whether vocal
or instrumental, is beautiful and full of meaning.

At a rehearsal I have stood in the chancel of some churches and
heard the complete tonal spectrum of a great organ or choir. But
when I walked halfway down the aisle, the tone deteriorated
progressively. What had happened was that the beautiful initial
tones were swallowed up in the millions of traps in cinderblock
walls of the chancel and auditorium or in the myriad miniature
recesses of pew cushions or in the deep piling of the carpets or in
the 760,925 holes in the ceiling blocks.

It was exactly as if I had admired an impressive painting of the Nativity or Crucifixion in the chancel; then, as I stood half-way back in the church, a vertical curtain of steam at the front of the chancel obscured the beauties of line and color.

During a service in such a church, when a hymn is announced and the singing begins I can hardly hear myself or my neighbor in the pew. We feel isolated from one another, yet we are a part of the worshiping congregation. The vocal acts of worship should be audible to each worshiper, helping him to know himself to be a part of the community of believers.

Can you have too much reflection, reverberation, and echo? Yes. Acoustical and architectural experts are able to determine the optimum point which is sympathetic to both speech and music.[2] It is important to attend to this matter, for it affects not only the ear of the expert but every layman who attends worship.

Wilmer T. Bartholomew in an excellent introductory text, *Acoustics of Music,* says:

> A certain amount of reverberation is useful in increasing the sound energy in the room. . . . if music be played in a room with too long a reverberation time the effect is similar to a piano being played with the damper pedal kept down, and the result is not only louder, but badly blurred. The reverberant sound in a hall may have a ratio as great as ten times that of the direct sound. If a lecturer is speaking we have difficulty in understanding him, since several syllables are always sounding at the same time. Increasing the loudness of the source may make matters worse instead of better. On the other hand, if the reverberation time is too short, the room seems too "dead," and speech and especially music become too crisp and *staccato,* a condition popularly termed *non-resonant.* This has a bad psychological effect on listeners as well as performers.[3]

CHAPTER **19** *Hymns in Church Camps, Conferences, and Conventions*

An increasing number of children, young people, and adults gather for brief periods in church-sponsored camps, conferences, and conventions. These co-operative ventures are usually high moments in the lives of those attending. The leadership is challenging and the fellowship is contagious. Those attending these assemblies return to their local congregations with a fresh insight and resolve.

Since these meetings do have strong direct influence on the life of local churches, it is indeed desirable that the hymnody of camps, conferences, and conventions be of a type which will not only reinforce the intent of these meetings but will be worth taking back home.

In young people's conferences especially we should make a clear distinction between the singing in the recreation periods and the singing in the services of worship. Young people love to sing popular fun songs, and sometimes music with this "flavor" is carried over to the more serious moments. An increasing number of conference song books are being issued with a wealth of healthy gay folk and fun songs, and, in addition, a collection of the fine hymns of the church.[1]

Summer camp experiences with youngsters can produce keen habits of hymn singing because intelligent leaders try to relate the actual daily happenings of camp life to their expression through song.

And our enormous church conventions—whether denominational or interdenominational—do feed back musical attitudes to the local church. Not only do conventions give opportunity for excellent congregational singing under skilled leadership, but worship experiences are frequently illumined by special choral and orchestral music. For example, the Methodist Church commissioned an oratorio for a national youth convention. It was "The Invisible Fire" based on hymn texts by Charles Wesley, with musical setting by Cecil Effinger.[2]

The Christian Church in Germany furnishes us with an example of the kind of musical influence we are advocating. At the Kirchentag where 500,000 people gathered for this annual event, a visitor describes the singing as follows:

> The singing here is on the very highest level, no catchy choruses with driveling words, but strong, objective theology set to robust and masculine tunes, the pick of the chorales, and especially commissioned modern music. There was a mass singing service this afternoon in Gruneburgpark that left one permanently enriched and strengthened.

CHAPTER **20** The Aids Offered
by the Hymn Society
of America

═══════════════════════════════

The Hymn Society of America is a national organization founded in 1922 to increase interest in Christian hymns and hymnology in America, and to raise the standards of hymns and hymn tunes and of their use by congregations.

How does the Society accomplish its purpose?

By cultivating the use of the best hymns and tunes.

By stimulating interest in congregational hymn singing.

By encouraging the writing and publication of hymns which express the spiritual needs of today.

By securing the production of hymn tunes of real musical value which lend themselves to effective congregational singing.

By collecting data on hymns; by promoting research, discussion, and writing in the field of hymnology; and by the occasional publication of such material.

What are the main activities of the Society?

Public meetings; hymn festivals; anniversary celebrations; new hymn and tune projects; publications, including the Society's Papers and *The Hymn*.

The Society endeavors to acquaint its members with the great hymns of the past, and also to promote the writing of new hymns and tunes to meet present needs.

What public meetings and services does the Society hold?

Each year, wherever the Society is established, it prepares local programs of meetings, open to the public, at which various phases of hymnody are presented and illustrated. Addresses by noted hymnologists at these meetings are frequently printed for distribution.

How does the Hymn Society share in the Hymn Festival movement?

This movement took definite shape in America through the efforts of the Society; and today such services are held over the country, often by large groups of churches which bring together their congregations and choirs for joint hymn festivals. They are frequently supported by local Chapters of the American Guild of Organists. They are primarily congregational in character, and have a profound effect on congregational singing and on the use of desirable new hymns and tunes.

What are anniversary celebrations?

The Society includes in its program nation-wide observances of great hymnic anniversaries, such as the Lowell Mason sesquicentennial in 1942, the Isaac Watts bicentennial in 1948, the 300th anniversary of the Scottish Psalter in 1950, the 400th anniversary of the Genevan Psalter in 1951, American Hymnody of the Twentieth Century in 1952, the Louis F. Benson 100th anniversary in 1955, the Charles Wesley 250th anniversary and the 150th Whittier anniversary, both in 1957. Hymn festivals, special church services, and public meetings are encouraged in commemoration of such occasions. As an aid to these events, leaflets containing both hymn texts and tunes, with annotations and other supplementary material, are available from the office of the Society.

What is THE HYMN?

The Hymn is a publication issued four times a year by the Society. It contains articles about hymns and their authors and composers. It also includes accounts of important activities of the Society and its members. *The Hymn* has been enthusiastically received since its first number in October 1949, and it may be found in numerous university and college libraries.

How does the Society encourage the writing of hymns?

It invites the submission of original hymns addressed to specific needs or to special occasions or to the general enrichment of hymnody. The most notable examples of recent new hymns are the "Eleven Ecumenical Hymns" prepared for use at the Evanston Assembly of the World Council of Churches in 1954; the "Five New Hymns on the City" prepared for the Convocation on Urban Life in America in 1954; and the "Ten New Hymns on the Bible" prepared for the celebration of the completion of the Revised Standard Version of the Bible in 1952. "Five New Hymns for Youth by Youth" and "Fourteen New Rural Hymns" were both published in 1955. Many of these hymns have had gratifying acceptance; and the ecumenical hymn by Georgia Harkness entitled "Hope of the World" has literally been sung around the world. To further encourage the writing of new hymns, the Society has inaugurated a plan which is called "Hymns of the Year." At the end of each year, new hymns received during the past twelve months are judged by a committee, and those deemed worthy are published. New tunes for the new texts are welcomed, especially where a new tune seems particularly needed.

May its members make use of Hymn Society source material?

Yes. They are invited to consult the valuable source material in its archives. This includes material collected by the Hymn Origins Committee, which has obtained statements direct from contemporary hymn writers about how their hymns came to be written.

In the Memorabilia Room in the Interchurch Center in New York will be found valuable hymnic and sacred music material.

The library of the Hymn Society is also a valuable source of material. The main portion of the library is housed at Union Theological Seminary in New York. The McAll Hymnic Collection is housed at the office of the Society.

THE AIDS OFFERED BY THE HYMN SOCIETY OF AMERICA

Does the Society answer queries relative to hymns and their use?

It renders a wide service through correspondence with individuals and organizations. This includes factual information in the field of hymnology and counsel regarding all aspects of hymnic activity. Those desiring information and assistance should communicate with the national office in New York.

Who are members of the Hymn Society?

The Society is glad to number among its members most of America's writers of hymns, hymnbook editors, and church musicians, both organists and choir directors, together with many ministers, Christian educators, and others. Its fellowship is open to *all those* interested in its objectives.

The national headquarters of the Society is in New York, but its members are found in almost every state of the Union. Those desiring to join the Society are invited to write the national office at 475 Riverside Drive, New York 27, New York. There is a special rate for the membership dues of students enrolled in schools of theology and sacred music. In addition, membership is open to institutions, such as the libraries of universities, departments of church music, theological seminaries, etc. This entitles them to all the current material issued by the Society.

Does the Hymn Society have local chapters?

Several local chapters of the Society have been organized to carry forward its purposes through their own programs, in cooperation with the national office. They can be formed wherever there are at least seven members of the Society. In several communities where there are less than seven members, "Committees" have been formed to carry on locally the work of the Society in anticipation of forming a chapter later.

What are the Papers of the Society?

They are monographs on a wide variety of hymnic subjects by competent authorities. Twenty-three Papers have thus far been published, and there are plans to add to their number in the near future. In addition to the Papers, reprints of important addresses, copies of new hymns and tunes secured by the Society, and current leaflets of hymns for hymn festivals and celebrations are forwarded to all members as they are published. A complete list of the Papers may be obtained from the office of the Society.

BIBLIOGRAPHY

•

NOTES AND ACKNOWLEDGMENTS

Bibliography

A. DICTIONARY

Julian, John, *A Dictionary of Hymnology*. First Edition 1892; Unabridged and unaltered republication of the 1907 revision, New York: Dover Publications, 1957.

B. BACKGROUND AND INTERPRETATION OF INDIVIDUAL HYMNS

1. *Handbooks*
    a. *American*

    Covert, W. C. and Laufer, Calvin W., *Handbook to The Hymnal*. (Presbyterian Church.) Philadelphia: Presbyterian Board of Christian Education, 1935.

    Haeussler, Armin, *The Story of Our Hymns*. (Evangelical and Reformed Church.) St. Louis: Eden Publishing House, 1952.

    McCutchan, Robert Guy, *Our Hymnody*. (Methodist Church.) New York: Abingdon Press, 1937, 1942.

    The Hymnal 1940 Companion, prepared by the Joint Commission on the Revision of the Hymnal of the Protestant Episcopal Church in the United States of America. New York: The Church Pension Fund, 1949, revised 1951.

    b. *British*

    Dearmer, Percy, *Songs of Praise Discussed*. London: Oxford University Press, 1933.

    Hymns Ancient and Modern. Historical edition with notes on the origin of both hymns and tunes, and a general historical introduction. London: William Clowes and Sons Ltd., 1909.

    Moffatt, James and Patrick, Millar, *Handbook to the Church Hymnary with Supplement*. London: Oxford University Press, 1935.

    Parry, K. L. and Routley, Erik, *Companion to Congregational Praise*. London: Independent Press Ltd., 1953.

2. *General Collections*

    Bailey, Albert Edward, *The Gospel in Hymns*. New York: Charles Scribner's Sons, 1950.

Benson, Louis F., *Studies of Familiar Hymns*, First and Second Series. Philadelphia: The Westminster Press, 1903, 1923.

MacKay, Ruth, *They Sang a New Song*. New York: Abingdon Press, 1959. (Written especially for children.)

Parry, Kenneth L., *Christian Hymns*. London: SCM Press Ltd., 1956.

Routley, Erik, *I'll Praise My Maker*. London: Independent Press Ltd., 1951.

Routley, Erik, *Hymns and the Faith*. Greenwich, Conn.: Seabury Press, 1956.

C. HISTORIES

1. *General*

Benson, Louis F., *The English Hymn: Its Development and Use in Worship*. Philadelphia: The Presbyterian Board of Publication, 1915.

Benson, Louis F., *The Hymnody of the Christian Church*. New York: George H. Doran Co., 1927. Reprinted 1956 by John Knox Press, Richmond, Va.

Gilman, F. J., *The Evolution of the English Hymn*. New York: The Macmillan Company, 1927.

Patrick, Millar, *The Story of the Church's Song*. Edinburgh: The Church of Scotland Committee on Publications, 1927, 1947. The American edition (1961, John Knox Press, Richmond, Va.) is illustrated by reference to *The Hymnbook* (Presbyterian) and *The Hymnal 1940* (Episcopal).

Phillips, C. S., *Hymnody Past and Present*. New York: The Macmillan Company, 1937.

Routley, Erik, *Hymns and Human Life*. London: John Murray, 1952.

2. *Special*

a. *German*

Liemohn, Edwin, *The Chorale through Four Hundred Years of Musical Development as a Congregational Hymn*. Philadelphia: Muhlenberg Press, 1953.

b. *Metrical Psalmody*

Patrick, Millar, *Four Centuries of Scottish Psalmody*. London: Oxford University Press, 1949.

c. *Watts and the Wesleys*

Bett, Henry, *The Hymns of Methodism*. London: The Epworth Press, 1945. (Revised edition.)

Davis, Arthur Paul, *Isaac Watts, His Life and Works*. New York: The Dryden Press, 1943.

Manning, Bernard L., *The Hymns of Wesley and Watts*. London: The Epworth Press, 1942.

Rattenbury, J. Ernest, *The Evangelical Doctrines of Charles Wesley's Hymns*. London: The Epworth Press, 1941, 1954.

Rattenbury, J. Ernest, *The Eucharistic Hymns of John and Charles Wesley*. London: The Epworth Press, 1948.

d. *American*

Ellinwood, Leonard, *The History of American Church Music.* New York: Morehouse-Gorham, 1953.

Foote, Henry Wilder, *Three Centuries of American Hymnody.* Cambridge: Harvard University Press, 1940.

e. *Carols*

Routley, Erik, *The English Carol.* New York: Oxford University Press, 1959.

D. MUSIC OF HYMNS

Frost, Maurice, editor, *English & Scottish Psalm & Hymn Tunes c. 1543-1677.* London: Oxford University Press, 1953.

McCutchan, Robert Guy, *Hymn Tune Names: Their Sources and Significance.* Nashville: Abingdon Press, 1957.

Routley, Erik, *The Music of Christian Hymnody. A study of the development of the hymn tune since the Reformation, with special reference to English Protestantism.* London: Independent Press Ltd., 1957.

E. CHURCH SCHOOL HYMNODY

Ingram, Madeline D., *Organizing and Directing Children's Choirs.* Nashville: Abingdon Press, 1959.

Jacobs, Ruth Krehbiel, *The Children's Choir.* Rock Island, Ill.: Augustana Press, 1958.

Morsch, Vivian S., *The Use of Music in Christian Education.* Philadelphia: The Westminster Press, 1956.

Thomas, Edith Lovell, *Music in Christian Education.* Nashville: Abingdon Press, 1953.

F. GENERAL CHURCH MUSIC BOOKS
(with sections on hymnody)

Davies, Walford and Grace, Harvey, *Music and Worship.* New York: The H. W. Gray Company, 1935.

Douglas, Winfred, *Church Music in History and Practice.* New York: Charles Scribner's Sons, 1937.

Halter, Carl, *The Practice of Sacred Music.* St. Louis: Concordia Publishing House, 1954.

Manual of Church Praise According to the Use of the Church of Scotland. Edinburgh: The Church of Scotland Committee on Publications, 1932.

Music in Church. The Report of the Committee appointed in 1948 by the Archbishops of Canterbury and York. London: Church Information Board, 1957. (Revised edition.)

Notes and Acknowledgments

Chapter 2—The Values of Congregational Singing

1. *The Journal of the Rev. John Wesley, A.M.*, edited by Nehemiah Curnock, Vol. I, pp. 142-143. (Slightly altered.) London: The Epworth Press, 1938.
2. From "Through the Night of Doubt and Sorrow" by Bernhardt S. Ingemann, 1825.
3. From "For All the Saints Who from Their Labors Rest" by William Walsham How, 1864.
4. I Corinthians 14:15.
5. From "My God and Father, While I Stray" by Charlotte Elliott, 1835.

Chapter 3—What Is Superior Congregational Singing?

1. Seven "Directions for Singing" appeared in the preface to his *Sacred Melody* of 1761. He included them in order that "this part of Divine Worship may be the more acceptable to God as well as more profitable" to singer and hearer. Those given here are quoted from *Manual of Church Praise According to the Use of the Church of Scotland*, pp. 147-148. Five of these "Directions" which pertain to modern congregations have been printed on a sheet for attachment to flyleaves of hymnals and for other uses. These may be purchased from Outlook Publishers, 512 East Main Street, Richmond 19, Virginia.
2. Walford Davies and Harvey Grace, *Music and Worship*, p. 141. New York: The H. W. Gray Company, 1935. Used by permission of Eyre & Spottiswoode (Publishers) Ltd., London.
3. Psalm 67:3.

Chapter 4—The Hymn: Text and Tune

1. James Moffatt and Millar Patrick, *Handbook to the Church Hymnary*, p. XIII. London: Oxford University Press, 1935. Used by permission.
2. Erik Routley, *The Music of Christian Hymnody*, p. 5. London: Independent Press Ltd., 1957. Used by permission.
3. C. S. Phillips, *Hymnody Past and Present*, p. 249. London: S.P.C.K., 1937. New York: The Macmillan Company. Used by permission.
4. Colossians 3:16.

5. Millar Patrick, *The Story of the Church's Song*, pp. 131-132. Edinburgh: The Church of Scotland Committee on Publications, 1927, 1947. Used by permission. (Revised edition available in 1961, published by John Knox Press, Richmond, Va.) See also Paper VI of The Hymn Society of America: *What is a Hymn?* by Carl Fowler Price.

6. See Index of Biblical References in *The Hymnal 1940 Companion* (Episcopal), p. 714; Index of Scripture Texts in *Our Hymnody* (Methodist), pp. 589-594; Index of Scriptural Allusions in *The Hymnbook* (Presbyterian 1955), pp. 551-554.

7. John Drinkwater, *The Muse in Council*, Being Essays on Poets and Poetry, p. 60. Boston: Houghton Mifflin Company, 1925. Used by permission of Sidgwick & Jackson Ltd., Bloomsbury Way, London.

8. Evelyn Underhill, *The Life of the Spirit and the Life of Today*, pp. 148-149. New York: E. P. Dutton & Company, 1922. London: Methuen & Co. Ltd. Used by permission of the author's executor and of the British and American publishers.

9. Quoted in Louis F. Benson, *The Hymnody of the Christian Church*, p. 112. Richmond, Va.: John Knox Press, 1956 (reprinted from the 1927 edition through arrangement with Harper & Brothers). This and other excerpts from this volume are used by permission.

10. From "Our God, to Whom We Turn" by Edward Grubb, 1925.

11. From "All Beautiful the March of Days" by Frances Whitmarsh Wile, 1912. Used by permission of Dorothy M. W. Bean.

12. See Carl Price's article on "Hymn Patterns" reprinted by The Hymn Society of America from *Religion in Life*, Summer, 1947.

13. John 14:6.

14. Henry Hallam Tweedy, "Eternal God, Whose Power Upholds," 1929. Used by permission of The Hymn Society of America.

15. *Music in Worship*: Report of the Archbishops' Committee appointed in 1922. Revised Edition 1938, p. 8. Reprinted by courtesy of the Church Information Office, Church House, Westminster, London, S.W. 1. (This volume is now out of print and has been superseded by *Music in Church*, revised 1957.)

16. This excerpt from DURROW is used by permission of The Educational Company of Ireland Limited, Dublin.

17. *Music in Worship*, pp. 7-8.

18. Benson, *op. cit.*, p. 148.

19. Routley, *op. cit.*, pp. 5-6.

20. From "Joyful, Joyful, We Adore Thee" by Henry van Dyke, 1907. Reprinted from *The Poems of Henry van Dyke* by permission of the publishers, Charles Scribner's Sons.

21. Robert Bridges, "About Hymns," p. 2. From *Occasional Papers*, No. II, Church Music Society. London: Oxford University Press, 1911. Used by permission of Church Music Society, Chipstead, Surrey.

22. Benson, *op. cit.*, p. 232.

Chapter 5—Basic Hymns Arranged Chronologically

1. Albert Bailey in his *The Gospel in Hymns* (Charles Scribner's Sons, 1950) uses these hymnals as bases for his studies of 313 hymns.

2. For other chronological lists of texts and tunes, see *The Hymnal 1940 Companion*, pp. XII-XIX; and in the hymnal *At Worship* (Harper & Brothers, 1951), see Index of Representative Hymns of the Ages, pp. 36-40.

3. Augustine, *The Confessions of Saint Augustine*, translated by E. B. Pusey, D.D., p. 213. Mount Vernon, N. Y.: Peter Pauper Press.

4. *Calvini Opera*, ed. 1863 seq., Vol. X a, 12. Listed in Benson, *The Hymnody of the Christian Church*, p. 80.

Chapter 6—Gospel Songs:
Their Influence on American Hymn Singing

1. Louis F. Benson, *The English Hymn*, p. 491. Philadelphia: The Presbyterian Board of Publication, 1915. Copyright 1915 by George H. Doran Company, New York.

2. Katherine Hankey, 1866.

3. Benson, *The Hymnody of the Christian Church*, pp. 266-267.

4. E. W. Blandly.

5. Ernest W. Shurtleff, 1888.

6. Fanny J. Crosby, 1868.

7. John 6:37.

8. William Walsham How, 1867.

9. Romans 8:38-39, R.S.V. This and other Scripture quotations from the Revised Standard Version are copyright 1946 and 1952 by Division of Christian Education of the National Council of the Churches of Christ in the United States of America.

10. K., in Rippon's *A Selection of Hymns*, 1787.

11. Harvey Grace, *The Complete Organist*, pp. 35-36. London: The Richards Press Ltd., 1920, 1950. Used by permission.

12. Waldo Selden Pratt, *Musical Ministries in the Church*, pp. 59-60 (paragraphing altered). New York: Fleming H. Revell Company, 1901. Used by permission.

Chapter 7—The Structure and Use of Hymnals

1. For debate on the desirability of having the music at the top of the page with the text printed as a poem at the bottom, see Dr. Benson's argument in *The Hymnody of the Christian Church*, pp. 220-224.

2. See especially Robert Guy McCutchan, *Hymn Tune Names: Their Sources and Significance*. Nashville: Abingdon Press, 1957.

3. From "Not Alone for Mighty Empire" by William Pearson Merrill, 1909. Used by permission.

Chapter 8—The Responsibility of the Leader of Worship
for Hymn Singing

1. See Bibliography for list of other handbooks.

2. F. J. Gillman, *The Evolution of the English Hymn*, p. 30. New York: The Macmillan Company, 1927. London: George Allen & Unwin Ltd. Used by permission.

3. The American edition of *The Story of the Church's Song* by Millar Patrick (John Knox Press, 1961) illustrates the text by reference to hymns

found in *The Hymnbook* (Presbyterian 1955) and *The Hymnal* 1940 (Episcopal).

4. Many pastors desire a comprehensive insight into the total area of church music. To assist such pastors, the author has prepared a brief reading course entitled "Church Music for the Pastor." This course is adaptable for a lay churchman also, and may be secured from the Library, Union Theological Seminary, 3401 Brook Road, Richmond 27, Va.

5. Joseph R. Sizoo, "Kindly Light," in *The Reader's Digest*, August 1945. Adaptation used by permission of author and publisher.

Chapter 9—The Playing of Hymns

1. This excerpt from LASST UNS ERFREUEN, found in *The English Hymnal*, has been reproduced by permission of Oxford University Press, London, England.

2. Hugh S. Roberton, *Mixed Voice Choirs*, p. 4. Glasgow: Paterson Sons & Co. Ltd. Used by permission.

3. *Manual of Church Praise* According to the Use of the Church of Scotland, p. 202. Edinburgh: The Church of Scotland Committee on Publications, 1932. Used by permission.

4. From "The Lord's My Shepherd, I'll Not Want," in *Scottish Psalter*, 1650.

5. From "In the Cross of Christ I Glory," by John Bowring, 1849.

6. Percy A. Scholes, *The Oxford Companion to Music*, p. 883. London: Oxford University Press, 1938.

7. As an example of processional interludes, see Dr. Richard Gore's setting of SINE NOMINE entitled "Festal Processional." (J. Fischer & Bro., No. 8504.)

8. See study document "The Church Organ," prepared by the Commission on Music, National Council of Churches, 475 Riverside Drive, New York 27, N. Y.

9. See also *Index to Hymn Preludes*, compiled by Martin H. Stellhorn. (Corcordia Publishing House.) This volume includes also postludes, voluntaries, paraphrases, variations, and other organ compositions, based on hymns, chorales, and carols. A listing of 2,200 selections of various publishers according to key, difficulty, and length.

Chapter 12—The Private Devotional Use of Hymns

1. Benson, *The Hymnody of the Christian Church*, p. 228.

2. *The Text Book of the Moravian Church*, Preface. Bethlehem, Pennsylvania, 1946.

3. William Cowper, 1779.

Chapter 13—Hymns in the Family Circle

1. Recounted in Millar Patrick's *The Story of the Church's Song*, p. 92. Used by permission.

2. An excellent brief (20 pages) introduction to family music is Public Affairs Pamphlet No. 260, *Time for Music—a guide for parents* by Beatrice Landeck. (Public Affairs Pamphlets, 22 East 38th St., New York 16, N. Y.)

3. *Songs of Praise*, Enlarged Edition, Nos. 399-405. London: Oxford University Press, 1931.

4. *Rejoice and Sing* is published for Presbyterian and Reformed Youth Fellowships and is available through their denominational bookstores.

5. Robert Burns, "The Cotter's Saturday Night," excerpts from stanzas XIII and XIX.

6. Benson, *The Hymnody of the Christian Church*, p. 276.

Chapter 14—Church School Hymnody

1. *Manual of Church Praise* According to the Use of the Church of Scotland, p. 242. Used by permission.

2. *Ibid.*, p. 245.

3. For guides in teaching hymns to choristers, see references to hymns in the indexes of Madeline Ingram's *Organizing and Directing Children's Choirs* and Ruth Krehbiel Jacob's *The Children's Choir*.

4. Archibald Alexander, *A Collection of Hymns*, New York, 1831. Quoted in Benson, *The Hymnody of the Christian Church*, pp. 148-149.

Chapter 15—How a Layman Learns a Hymn

1. Frances Whitmarsh Wile, 1912. By permission.

2. From an address, "Organ Accompaniment for Congregational Singing," given before The Hymn Society of America by Professor Ray F. Brown. Used by permission.

Chapter 16—Congregational Rehearsals

1. Davies and Grace, *Music and Worship*, p. 145.

2. Harry Plunket Greene, *Interpretation in Song*, pp. 37-144 (brief excerpts). London: Macmillan & Co. Ltd., 1912, 1931. New York: St. Martin's Press, Inc. Used by permission.

3. For instruction in leading informal singing see Eisenberg, *How to Lead Group Singing* (Association Press); and Frieswyk, *Forty Approaches to Informal Singing* (National Recreation Association).

4. Davies and Grace, *op. cit.*, p. 147.

5. Hymn quiz (abbreviated) is reproduced from *The Presbyterian Outlook* by permission of the author, Dr. Kenneth J. Foreman.

Chapter 17—Hymn Services and Festivals

1. This order of worship, prepared by the Reverend Philip S. Watters, is included by permission of The Hymn Society of America.

2. Help in dating these services can be had from "A Hymn Calendar" in *Our Hymnody* (Methodist handbook), pp. 569-584. This hymn calendar gives the days of each month of the year with the birth and death dates of leading hymnological figures.

Chapter 18—Acoustics and Its Effect on Congregational Singing

1. Sir James Jeans, *Science & Music*, p. 212. Cambridge: Cambridge University Press, 1937, 1947. Used by permission of the American Branch, New York.

2. See Briefs for Church Builders, Number 4, "Arrangements for Music," and Number 8, "Sound Control," prepared by the Department of Church

823a

t w

Building, National Council of Churches, 475 Riverside Drive, New York 27, N. Y.

See also Pamphlet Number 4, "Acoustics and the Musician," and Pamphlet Number 13, "Sound—Its Significance in Worship," both by Ray Berry, published by American Guild of Organists, 630 Fifth Avenue, New York 20, N. Y.

3. Wilmer T. Bartholomew, *Acoustics of Music*, p. 69. New York: Prentice-Hall, Inc., 1942, 1950.

Chapter 19—Hymns in Church Camps, Conferences, and Conventions

1. See *Rejoice and Sing*, published for Presbyterian and Reformed Youth Fellowships and available through their denominational bookstores.

A good vest-pocket-size hymnal for men's gatherings is *Songs for Men*. (John Knox Press, Richmond, Va.)

International ecumenical gatherings usually use the multilingual *Cantate Domino*. (World's Student Christian Federation.)

2. A recording of "The Invisible Fire" may be purchased through the Methodist Board of Education, Box 871, Nashville 2, Tennessee.